CLOSE
CALLS

CLOSE
CALLS

Memoirs of a Survivor

FELICIA
BERLAND
HYATT

HOLOCAUST LIBRARY
An imprint of the
UNITED STATES HOLOCAUST MEMORIAL MUSEUM
WASHINGTON, D.C.

This reprint is published by the United States Holocaust Memorial Museum, 100 Raoul Wallenberg Place, SW, Washington, D.C. 20024-2126.

Cover photos: *(top)* USHMM, courtesy of Philip Vock; *(middle, from left)* Felicia Berland Hyatt; National Archives; Felicia Berland Hyatt; Glowna Komisja Badania Zbrodni Przeciwko Narodowi Polskiemu; National Archives. Back cover: *(top)* USHMM, courtesy of National Archives; *(author photo)* Samantha Sierra. Title page: USHMM, courtesy of National Archives.

ISBN 0-89604-138-7

Typeset by Duke & Company, Devon, Pennsylvania
Printed by Victor Graphics, Inc.

Printed in the United States of America

I dedicate this book to my mother, Sara Hilf Berland,

and to my father, Abraham Berland,

whose parenting made it possible for me to survive.

Contents

Acknowledgments

THANKS ARE DUE to a great many people for the help and support they have given me in setting down my painful recollections of the Nazi Holocaust.

I wish to thank Sol Lewis, executive editor of Holocaust Publications, who patiently and painstakingly supported this project.

I am also deeply indebted to Dr. Martin Pope, president of the Ezra Jack Keats Foundation, for his personal and official support.

I thank Deborah Judith Pope, the founder/artistic director of The New Theater of Brooklyn, for making it possible for me to present my story to the public as part of the theater's oral history series.

Among others who helped are Louis Falstein, Ruth Dropkin, Louis Heitner, Drs. Sheila and Richard White, Dr. Philip Zeigler, Noraleen Gutterman, and Alene Grossman. Many others, too numerous to list here, were very helpful in many ways, and I thank them as well. I cannot overlook thanking Ellen Gibbs, Lillian Sarno, Cele Klein, Anna Ternbach, Kenneth Miller, Peter Berland, Irving and Esther Rabb, Leah and Bea Kimmelman, Jack and Mary Ireland, and Fela Blechman. Special thanks are due to Steven Frohlich and Eileen Fischer of B.F. Graphics.

Foreword

THIS IS THE STORY of a Holocaust survivor, and, as such, it is a precious record and warning of the depravity that can take over the government and the people of seemingly civilized nations.

On another level, it is a thriller: a story of chases, escapes, close calls, cloak-and-dagger situations, breathtaking strategies, and suspense enough to rival fiction.

It is the account of a young Jewish woman who was born in Chelm, Poland, in 1920, the same Chelm that evokes a smile as one recalls the charming folktales of Eastern Europe. In September 1939, at the point of migrating to Bolivia, her escape route was cut off by Hitler's invasion of Poland. Her life thereafter was filled with harrowing adventures, the penalty for a misstep being death or imprisonment. She worked as a maid for an SS man, was saved from suicide and death by a long series of small miracles culminating in her imprisonment in Auschwitz. By breathtaking daring, she escaped from that death camp, ending up in a Czech labor camp. Finally, the war ended. The reaction of the prisoners to their newfound freedom provides revealing and frightening insights into the potentials of self-destructive behavior of those who are oppressed.

Strangely and rather amazingly, this is not a depressing story. It has all the tension and excitement usually associated with an action-packed novel.

Felicia Berland Hyatt is still spunky, bright, and optimistic. Her story had to be told.

Lillie Pope, Ph.D.

Preface

I HAVE WRITTEN MY STORY because I believe that all of us who survived the Nazi occupation have an obligation to record the circumstances under which we lived and came through. I am getting older, as are all the survivors. Soon there will be few, if any, of us alive to attest to what really happened. Recently there has been an alarming upsurge of denial and a tendency to forget the events that occurred. It is of the utmost importance that our experiences be recorded as a warning for posterity.

Fortunately, there are individuals who are consumed with the urgency to tell the story of these dark days, even though they themselves were never the direct victims of such persecution. Such an individual is Dr. Lillie Pope, and I have had the good fortune to know her.

Although she has always insisted that her efforts require no grateful acknowledgment, that her efforts reflect her duty, obligations, and social responsibility as a moral human being, it is necessary to make note of her contribution.

Dr. Pope heard my story, encouraged me to record it, and provided audiences to listen to me. She insisted that I make a large investment of my time to write my story; she made a similar investment of her time in interviewing me, recording, editing, and supervising additional editing. She made the necessary arrangements for having this book published, and followed up every detail carefully and tenaciously. Without her involvement, there would never have been any book. Such a contribution must be recognized.

GROWING UP IN CHELM

I WAS BORN IN POLAND in an ancient town called Chelm. Jewish settlers are reported to have come to Chelm during the twelfth century.

One of the oldest Slavic settlements, Chelm became a bishopric of the Eastern Orthodox Church in the thirteenth century. Chelm passed to Poland in 1377, to Austria in 1795, and to Russia in 1815. Chelm returned to Poland in 1921. It is a railway center, a trading center, and it manufactured metals, farm tools, and liquors.

In 1827, Chelm had a population of 2,793, of whom 1,902 were Jewish; by 1931, the population numbered 29,074, including 13,537 who were Jewish. In 1939, Jews numbered approximately 15,000, about fifty percent of the town's population.

Chelm has a special place in the hearts, humor, and culture of Yiddish-speaking Jews. Like Gotham in England and Schildburg in Germany, Chelm, for some unaccountable reason, has been the focus of irreverent folklore which satirizes the naiveté and stupidity of the population.

The stories about the fools of Chelm have a special flavor and coloring. They have Jewish settings and illuminate many facets of Jewish irony and wit. They unquestionably constitute an original body of folklore.[1] The very mention of Chelm conjures warmth and humor.

The Jewish community of Chelm was in existence for roughly seven hundred years. There were fifteen thousand Jews in Chelm when the Germans invaded Poland in 1939. The Nazis declared Chelm *Judenrein*[2] on November 6, 1942. Not a single Jew resides in Chelm at this time.

I was an only child and so was my mother. In contrast, my father was one of nine children, all of whom grew up and worked in the family bakery. Most of them opened bakeries of their own after they started their own families. I was born in

---

1. Nathan Ausubel, *A Treasury of Jewish Folklore,* Crown Publishers, N.Y., 1948.
2. Without Jews

1920, about a year after my father opened his bakery, and at the same time that Poland regained its independence following years of oppression and rule by four conquering countries: Russia, Prussia, Germany, and Austria. During World War I my father served in the Russian and later the Polish army. Thus he took part in the fight for Poland's independence, and with new opportunities for economic growth, my father took advantage of the situation. He started in a modest way and through the years his business flourished.

During my childhood, we lived in a non-Jewish neighborhood. I was raised with children whose parents were staunch Catholics, and, as a neighbor, I was treated quite well by the children. We played together and visited each other, but every now and again I experienced some teasing from my very best friends who never let me forget that I was Jewish. For example, I remember, as a very young child, that the brother of one of my close friends tried to push a piece of ham down my throat. At that time, my maternal grandmother lived with us and my mother kept a kosher home; we did not eat ham. I was very frightened; I thought I would die when that piece of ham went down my throat. I vomited, and I had to be given a great deal of reassurance from my grandmother and my parents that God would not punish me. The boy's mother beat him in front of the house in the presence of all the neighbors.

As part of my friendship with the Polish children, I was able to learn about Catholic religious observances and culture. I was invited to participate in the celebration of Catholic holidays, and I was frequently taken to church by a Catholic housekeeper who worked for us. Later on we employed a young woman who was Greek Orthodox to help in the home; both of them would take me to church. When the maid took me there, it was done secretly, as I was afraid my grandma would berate me. Because of these visits, I learned some of the prayers, rituals, and regulations that would serve me in good stead later.

Financially, my family was fairly comfortable, and I usually received whatever I wanted as a child, in terms of material things.

My mother was a very busy woman. She worked in the retail section of the bakery while my father was busy organizing all sorts of wholesale enterprises. He had many soldier friends with whom he had served in the army during the First World War and, consequently, was able to gain entrance into the army base that was located just outside of our town. Because of this, we were able to profit a great deal financially, as my father was the only licensed wholesaler for most government institutions in Chelm. The bakery was open all days of the week. The retail annex operated six and a half days. On Sundays, blue laws were observed and the store closed at noon when church services would begin. However, latecomers could enter the store through the back door. Policemen watching that the law be obeyed were not averse to taking bribes to look the other way.

Some rather unpleasant events occurred when I was a little girl of about three or four. At that time, my mother became seriously ill; I later found that her appendix had burst. She had not been treated properly by the doctor and the local hospital could not take care of her. She therefore had to be taken by train and ambulance to Lublin, the larger town near Chelm. My father was told that she was not going to survive. I recall very distinctly how he prepared me to say goodbye to my mother. They dressed me in my holiday best, a beautiful dress and a little black velvet coat. I was not told very much, but I sensed that it was a very solemn occasion because my father usually did not bother dressing me and buttoning my coat. He set me on the huge mahogany dining room table, and told me to remain calm. Instead, I felt a very weird sensation.

We went to Lublin where my mother's cousins lived, and we stayed with them. Then my father took me to the hospital, and upon arriving, found that my mother was no longer in her room but was out in the corridor. There was a little curtain drawn around her bed. Somehow though, when I arrived, she opened her eyes and reached out to me. I stood there for a while and then the nurse led me away. When we came back the next day, my mother was out of danger and was back in her room. Apparently the surgery was successful and she survived. But for years afterwards, she suffered as a result of this emergency surgery. It seems that when they did the final suturing, her fallopian tubes became attached to her stomach wall. They discovered this many years later when she wanted to become pregnant; my father wanted a son, and she was unable to conceive.

From the age of four until I was about seven, I would travel a great deal with my mother when she went to the "big specialists" in Cracow and many other places. I also accompanied her when they sent her to the spas. She eventually did conceive but she had to be rushed to Warsaw where they discovered that the botched original surgery in Lublin was the source of her trouble. This, I believe, was a disappointment for my parents: my mother could not give my father the heir he wanted.

During my youth, the inhabitants of Chelm numbered about 30,000, with a large Jewish population totaling almost half. The Jews were primarily involved in commerce and in services. They owned dry goods stores, and were shoemakers and dressmakers. Twice a week during market days Polish peasants from surrounding villages would come to town to sell their produce and to buy supplies. I loved to go to market.

There were several Jewish doctors, one non-Jewish doctor, a few Jewish dentists, and an optometrist in town. There was also one Jew who was a physician's aide and the people had more faith in him than they did in the doctor because he usually recommended effective home remedies.

Some Jews were fairly well-to-do although there were many poor ones as well. There was one area where the impecunious Jews lived; they earned their living as peddlers, selling all kinds of wares. Jewish teachers worked in Jewish schools only. In order to teach in state-sponsored schools, some Jewish teachers converted to Catholicism.

Many of the non-Jewish people in Chelm were employed in government services, as was our neighbor with whose children I played. He was a train engineer. Many stores were owned and managed by Poles. They also worked as builders and laborers. There were Polish bakers and non-Polish ones, although the crafts people were mostly Jewish. There were also shoemakers and the like who were not Jewish. My mother's cousin came to live in Chelm; she was a midwife and her husband was a government worker. I had a friend whose father was a notary public, and a paralegal aide. The more attractive stores were not owned by Jews; there was a flour mill, a cement and brick factory, and a brewery which were owned by Jews. Poles worked in the hospitals and served as teachers.

My maternal grandmother lived with us and had a very special way to try to stop me from doing the things she didn't think I should do. She was not like my mother, who would put her foot down, tell me to stop doing something, and mean it. My grandma would usually tell me a little story. For instance, when she didn't want me to speak disrespectfully about other people, she would tell me that if I talked unfavorably about others, they would start to hiccup and would never be able to stop. She also said that if I talked about people, their ears would burn. Another thing I used to do was to make funny faces or cross my eyes and make all kinds of crazy gestures. She told me that one day I'd get caught in a draft and remain permanently cross-eyed.

Before we moved to our own home, which was built for us in 1931, we resided in an apartment building. We lived upstairs and a Polish family was our next door neighbor. The landlord's quarters were above us and in the basement were two Jewish shoemakers and their large families, both quite poor, in one room, and with many children who were usually not supervised. They were always running around in the street. Our building was located on the main road, a major thoroughfare always crowded with lots of horses and horse-drawn wagons that came in from the country. Crossing the street was very dangerous and I was always told not to do so. But the kids from downstairs were daring and they wouldn't wait for anyone to lead them across. One girl who was my age became my playmate.

When her mother called her, she would scream so loudly that everyone in the street could hear her. There was a meadow across the road where we used to play, and when those kids were crossing the main thoroughfare, their mother would run after them shouting and cursing them "You should drop dead," but at the same time warn them to be careful and not to get killed. As a child, I could not understand why she wished them to drop dead. This was something I had not heard at home, and so when I did, for the first time, it struck me as very peculiar.

I had lots of toys and was rather bossy as a child, but when my friends were nice to me I would allow them to come to my house so that we could play together. When they weren't friendly I would take all my things away. I can see now how mean that was since those kids really did not have anything.

Since there was no central water system in Chelm, a well had to be drilled in the backyard of our newly built house and every morning the boys who worked in the bakery had to pump the water up to the tank in the attic. When we lived in the rented apartment, as well as in the new home, there were wood-burning stoves. The wood was chopped in the backyard and my father taught me how to do this. In the new house my parents allowed me to help pump the water with one of the workers. We had two horses and a dog in the backyard of our new home. For a long time there was no real pavement leading to our house and after the rain we were unable to dress to go anywhere, because the street was very muddy and we had to use wooden planks on large stones to avoid getting dirty. Since I was usually in a hurry I often slipped and fell into the mud. On the whole, though, it was a very comfortable home.

Our house was a fairly large two-story brick structure. The bakery was located on the ground floor. It was very roomy, modern, and largely mechanized, with many big windows. The floors were made of cement which, at my mother's suggestion, was mixed with brick-colored paint. In the main and largest hall where the dough was prepared, my mother designed a sort of walkway made of colored ceramic tiles, which she personally matched and inserted into the soft brick-colored cement. I can still see her on her hands and knees perched on a makeshift scaffold, arranging the small black-and-white tiles.

Our living quarters were on the first floor and consisted of a large L-shaped kitchen with built-in closets, cupboards, and a buffet. There were two bedrooms, one for my parents and one for me. My maternal grandmother slept in the kitchen and so did the maid who made her little space on the same end of the L in the kitchen. Two colorful curtains, a small table, and two chairs separated the two beds. We also had a very large living/dining room in which were a huge mahogany dining table, two oversized cedar closets, a sofa, and a buffet. We had no garden, but there were two balconies furnished with all sorts of plant and flower boxes. The bathroom was near the kitchen area. Our backyard housed a stable for our two horses, a barn for the delivery van, and a wheel wagon which we would convert into a sleigh for winter.

My parents were very much involved socially. There was no permanent theater in our town when I was a small girl, but national troupes did come through. My parents took me to see every form of entertainment that came to town; I saw Morris Turkov and Ida Kaminska. I remember many of the plays, and particularly one where somebody shot himself: I was watching with a cousin and we hid under the chair; that's how frightened we were. We saw the Dzigan and Schumacher comedians. When I considered myself grown-up, I stopped accompanying my parents to the Jewish theater. It was not seemly for a *gimnazistka*[3] to go to the Jewish Theater, I thought at the time. But then the movies came to town; there were only two at the beginning, one centrally located and the other a little out of town. I recall seeing a few Polish operas on film, and several Polish and foreign plays, the latter in translation.

My parents considered it quite important that I be given the best education possible. There was one private kindergarten in the entire city of Chelm and my mother paid the tuition for me to attend. I remember the teacher, and in particular her male friend. He had long hair made into a big braid which he wore inside the back of his shirt collar like the Chinese. He was a peculiar kind of fellow. Mrs. Gibalska, the head mistress, was an excellent teacher, very conscientious, and very good with children. I am a little hazy about whether this was a private school for Jewish children only, as I recall only Jewish classmates. Of about thirty kindergarten children from that group, I know of only two who survived: a gentleman who now lives in Israel and a woman who resides in San Francisco.

At the time I attended kindergarten, my mother decided that Palestine was our future and Hebrew should be our language. She had a friend who belonged to the same organization that she did. This man was a writer, but he didn't earn a living and so she hired him. He taught me Hebrew when I was about five years old. I learned to speak that language and became quite popular. Wherever I went, I was asked to say something in Hebrew. This man left for Israel in the late 1920s and I forgot everything I had learned.

When the time came for me to enter primary school, my parents selected a special one, not the regular public school that the other children attended. It was a state-sponsored teachers' seminary attached to a public school so that the students

---

3. Secondary school student or graduate

who were studying to become teachers had access to our classes to observe and practice their future calling. It was a very special place and it set me apart from my neighborhood playmates, as not everyone could afford the fees. I attended this school from the first to the seventh grades. Here we wore a uniform: a brown pleated skirt with an over-blouse and a black apron (of the type that is now worn in the kitchen). We wore this in the summer and winter; however those who could afford it had a lighter weight uniform for the summer and a winter one made of heavier woolen material.

This school was quite a long walk from my home. Writers speak of the hill upon which Chelm was built, and my school was midway down this peak. I have fond memories of winter play there. We wore backpacks and used these as sleds to ride down the incline during lunchtime when we would sneak out of school. It was dangerous because the streets were in poor condition and we had to compete with the traffic. Some accidents were unavoidable, but no one paid much attention to that. We had lots of fun during the winter.

An important part of the school curriculum was the teaching of religion. However, when the Catholic students studied this subject, we who were Jewish usually had that time off and would go out into the garden. The Jewish students attended religion classes before the regular school day started, from seven to eight a.m. This meant that during the wintertime it was pitch dark outside when we marched off to school. I was dressed properly for this, as my parents could afford the tall laced shoes and leggings that reached up to my knees.

Our Jewish religion teacher was a well-educated Russian and his Polish accent was horrendous. We used to have a lot of fun at his expense because of this, but he taught us well. He was strict, but he knew his subject: Jewish history, the Ten Commandments and whatever else pertained to our Jewish heritage and daily lives.

By and large, however, the atmosphere in this school was definitely anti-Semitic. For instance, one of the things the teachers insisted upon was that Yiddish not be spoken at home. They considered it a harsh language with hard consonants which affected the inflection in the Polish language. As for myself, I had no difficulty in speaking Polish at home because we had many Polish peasants working for us in the bakery as well as a Polish maid. My grandmother spoke the language although she preferred Yiddish. She would talk Yiddish to me and I would answer in Polish. My parents never told me that this was wrong, but now I realize that it was wrong not to have maintained our own language; at the time I saw nothing wrong with it.

Our school week included compulsory attendance on Saturdays, and in spite of our home being strict in regard to Jewish Sabbath observance, I did attend. This caused a problem with my paternal grandmother as she became quite angry when she would see me walking by her house on Saturday on the way to school. Our class session lasted until twelve on Saturdays, and the only concession the school made to the Jewish students was that we were not required to write on Saturdays.

Later on, my mother hired a *melamed*[4] to instruct me in prayers and to continue to teach me to read Yiddish and Hebrew. I hated those lessons because I was the only one in the entire neighborhood who had a Yiddish tutor. All the other kids would be out playing while I sat at home studying. I remember things that this melamed used to tell me. I was very impatient, sitting on a chair from which my feet couldn't reach the floor, so I would swing my legs back and forth. He considered this a distraction and, like my grandmother, he always said something to stop me. He warned me that if I didn't cease swinging my legs, something dire would happen to my parents. I asked how anything could possibly happen to them when they were at some other place and I was here. He said that my energetic leg movements were tantamount to cursing them; and so I would stop.

All of my home tutoring stopped when I entered primary school where they advised the parents to stop teaching Yiddish to their children. Because I attended this special school, I became very selective about the kids with whom I associated. I seldom played with the shoemaker's children in the courtyard, and when I did, I was always afraid that someone might see me with them.

When the time came for me to transfer from the grammar school to the *gimnazium* my parents began inquiring about admissions. To get into the government-financed gimnazium, one had to be a top-notch student. There was a quota: only four Jewish students would be accepted into each class. There were eight classes in gimnazium. One through three used a single curriculum; four through eight used two curricula, humanistic and scientific. Passing a difficult entrance examination was required. Professor Jaworski who taught at that school and who also did preparatory tutoring, was on the Board of Admissions and his fee was high. The professor taught about ten Jewish students, all competing for the eight openings. Everyone knew that all ten would not be admitted, but they nevertheless paid him an exorbitant amount of money. It amounted to one hundred zlotys weekly, and he tutored us for the examination for about six weeks. The pressure was enormous but my mother knew how important the coaching was and we could afford it.

I did pass the entrance examination but I placed tenth. I was out. I was heartbroken and so were my parents. The professor offered a compromise. He suggested that I accept admission into the third, instead of the fourth grade. I ob-

---

4. Teacher

jected, but the prospect of going through the same process next year was not too pleasant either. After some discussion with my parents and conferences with the professor, I reluctantly accepted the compromise solution and I entered the lower grade in September of 1933.

I was thirteen years old when I enrolled in the third grade and I enjoyed a marvelous year. I was a star student, received all As, and all sorts of awards, which buoyed my confidence. At that point the third grade was not yet divided into scientific and humanistic sections; we therefore took all sorts of tests to determine to which division we would be assigned, and I came out fifty-fifty. In the humanities division they taught Greek and Latin in addition to other languages, and I decided I did not want to study languages, I therefore enrolled in the scientific section because I was good at mathematics in the third grade and my math teacher discouraged me from entering the humanities department. I was sorry afterwards; we studied more physics, chemistry, and geology. I grew to dislike these subjects in the more advanced classes.

The school was very strict about punctuality. A Catholic prayer was recited each morning at the start of the first class and at the end of the last one. The Jewish children did not participate; instead, we were supposed to chant our own. Listening to the prayers over the years I learned the Catholic ones.

I made very good friends during the first year of school and we remained very close until our schooling was over. Since we were singled out as Jewish children, the friendships which were formed were mostly among our Jewish peers. A group of five of us formed a particularly close bond: we called ourselves a Quintumvirate. There were four Jewish girls and one who was not Jewish, who used to live in my old neighborhood, before we moved to our new house. She always joined us wherever we went and whatever we were doing. One of those five girls was my very close and dear friend, Henia. I was called Felka when I was young. We were inseparable and the kids would tease us calling us both Sonja Henia.

A little later on, boys entered the picture. It was a mixed group in that there were only two Jewish boys in our class, and the rest were Polish[5] who sometimes joined us. We had exceptionally good times then. We stayed out of school occasionally, which was very unusual for the Jewish students, but I suppose pressure of our peers succeeded in making us truant. We would arrive at school and then sneak out into the back streets, into the meadows or wherever, so that we could be like everybody else.

Despite the closeness that formed with some of the non-Jewish boys and girls,

---

5. When I say Polish, I mean non-Jewish.

we also experienced a number of anti-Semitic incidents and harassings. These took place mainly in the cloakrooms, which were located in the basement of the huge school building. We had to leave our coats downstairs. When I was about sixteen, my mother bought me a fur coat. It was, I suppose, a status symbol for her; for me however it was a source of difficulties because the kids would tease me about it.

One day, going down to the cloakroom for my coat, I failed to find it on my hanger. As I looked around I noticed two boys holding it as if to help me put it on. Before I knew it, they threw it over my head, rolled me on the floor, beat and kicked me. When I got up, someone behind me urged me not to report the incident to the teachers because I would be pummeled again. I left the school quite disheveled and, since the teachers were always particular as to how we looked, one of them approached me and asked me what happened. I said nothing, and of course, she suspected that there had been an incident. This was the homeroom teacher and when she entered the room the next day, she said that she had seen someone who had walked out on the previous day looking very upset. She invoked the honor of the students to explain what had happened. No one admitted to anything, but eventually they did say, "You know, we were just horsing around." But it was not true. These things happened fairly often. No matter how friendly we were with the non-Jewish kids, there was always something they would do to upset us, later insisting that it was all in fun.

When it came to playing pranks on the teachers, the Jewish children would participate. We used to tease them, we would put chalk on their chairs so their clothing would get dirty, we would bring frogs, beetles, snakes, and the like and turn them loose on the teachers.

As I think back to my school years, I remember the good times, the bad times, and mostly the uneasy ones, the latter occasioned by the fact that we, the Jewish kids, never knew what to expect even from our good friends who were not Jewish. Most of this was probably due to the fact that they often acted out the bad attitudes and prejudices of their elders. Whenever the economic situation became bleak, the Jews were blamed. Incidents of beatings or teasings of the Jewish youngsters usually increased during specific periods such as the Passover holidays. Many of the Poles in our city actually believed that the Jews needed the blood of the Polish children to prepare their matzohs. This canard was so prevalent that somehow they always managed to produce a dead Polish child, alleging that the Jews killed him or her. I distinctly remember the dread and anger I felt during such times. I truly believe that these stories were fabricated for the sole purpose of perpetuating their religious prejudices.

Attending gimnazium also created other problems. We, the students, considered ourselves intellectually superior to those attending other schools in Chelm, and there were several good ones in our town. There was a secondary commercial school, two teacher seminaries, one for men and the other for women, and also a Jewish gimnazium. But we considered ourselves the elite and we didn't usually associate with those attending the other learning institutions. They, I suppose suffered the same anti-Semitic treatment. As a result, Jewish youth formed clubs that were exclusively Jewish. We did not join those organizations until we were much older, perhaps seventeen or eighteen. Until then, those of us attending the gimnazium kept to ourselves. The Jewish youth groups arranged lots of parties and dances which were important socially, and that's when we veered away from our gimnazium group. But the five girls continued to be close to each other.

During the summers, there weren't camps to go to, and so we planned our own fun. My father had a horse and wagon, and used it for outings. He adored children and all the kids on the block used to follow him around. On Sundays, when he was free, he used to gather all the neighborhood children, and me and my friends. He would take us on picnics in the forests, and on trips to neighboring villages.

I have pleasant recollections of the sleigh rides on which my father took us. During the winter my father would sometimes arrange for a mock breakdown of the sleigh that would spill all of us into a ditch which was filled with snow.

During the school year, part of the program was devoted to learning about the Polish countryside and to taking trips out of our town. Those who could afford it would pay for those school trips, and those who weren't able to, received some sort of scholarship. As a result, I learned a great deal about many large cities in Poland. This was a very good agenda. It also imbued us with an appreciation of art, because whenever we visited another large city we were taken to museums and concerts and other cultural events. During the summer and winter, some entertainment group would come to town and we would also attend their concerts.

We all complained about the hard work we did, and that we didn't like school; we couldn't wait for the school year to end. In retrospect they were really pleasant, exciting, fun years.

Chapter 1

ATTEMPT TO EMIGRATE

THE ECONOMIC SITUATION had changed for my parents while I was in gimnazium. In the 1930s news of some of Hitler's nefarious activities were already filtering through to us and one of the Polish ministers named Beck was asked whether it would be all right to take business away from the Jews. Beck replied, "Well, I don't know whether it would be proper, but if you want to organize a boycott, that would be all right. Constitutionally you cannot take the business away." The Jewish firms were therefore already being boycotted. More and more Polish people established businesses and supplanted most of the occupations previously held by Jews. Pilsudski, who was the first Premier of Poland, decided to resettle many Polish railroad workers from the West to Chelm because it had been under Russian domination for many years. He wanted to make it more Polish. He therefore proceeded to expand the railroad station of Chelm so that people from other parts of Poland would come and live in this town.

My father was a very active member of the community. He was president of the Bakers' Guild and so he frequently traveled to Lublin and to Warsaw as a Guild representative. He was also active in many Jewish charitable and other organizations. When we became a little more financially independent, the tax department in Chelm chose him to be a tax assessor of Jewish small businessmen. It was a terrible position. Many Saturdays there was a line of people extending all the way through the living room into the bedroom of our home. They came to plead for exemptions from taxation. He was to speak for the Jewish businessmen, and he hated that task, which was essentially a guessing game about other people. He would be asked to estimate how much people earned. In the end, the government alone would levy the taxes, but he felt responsible and he knew that he had made many enemies because the small businessmen blamed him for their tax rates.

As a representative of the Guild, he sometimes spoke on behalf of his organization in the Senate and the Congress. As a result, he met many people who later were helpful to him when we were in trouble and who assisted him in emigration.

About 1936, a downward economic trend plagued our town. The Polish government began zeroing in on the Jewish businesses. Even though it had as yet not confiscated anything, it tacitly encouraged a policy of non-support for the Jews. That's when my parents were confronted with their first dire economic problems, because government-operated agencies started cutting their orders to Jewish business people. We had to scale down the business, but we could not reduce the costs of electricity or heating or the number of workers we required.

At that point, my parents needed to borrow some money. The only acceptable collateral was their house. They found a young Jewish couple with two children who loaned them a sum of money and moved into a part of our house. The rent covered the interest on our loan. This necessitated our dividing the apartment which we occupied on top of the bakery. I had to give up my bedroom as did my parents, and another kitchen was installed in one of the hallways for the new family. Our living quarters were then on one side, and they were quite compact.

My parents were very irritable and the money they borrowed did not last long because expenses continued to mount. My father began thinking of selling everything and leaving Poland. He felt terribly hurt when the people who were in charge of ordering, like the master sergeants of the army base who had been his friends since they fought together for the liberation of Poland, would stop buying from him. They kept explaining that their orders came from above, and that they could do nothing about it. What the army friends did suggest was a sharing proposition. A Polish bakery would deliver half their needs, and my father would deliver the other half. My father's share soon dwindled to one-quarter and then even less. It thus became impossible to operate our bakery. This reinforced my father's resolve to emigrate.

He had two brothers in New York and one in Australia. The American quota was closed for the Polish population, Polish Jews in particular. So he wrote to his brother in Melbourne, Australia, asking him to send us the necessary immigration papers for my mother, myself, and for him. His brother, of course, was cooperative.

My maternal grandmother, who lived with us all my life, could not be included in my parents' plan to emigrate to Australia because she was not a blood relative of my father's brother who undertook to send us immigration affidavits. Needless to say, this was a very upsetting development to all of us, especially to my grandmother, who was first inconsolable. Eventually my mother succeeded in calming her down by assuring her that, as her daughter, she would be able to send for her six months after our arrival in Australia.

A family crisis soon ensued, because my father's oldest brother, my paternal grandmother, and my father's youngest sister and her husband also owned bakeries in Chelm; there were three Berland bakeries in the city. Ours was quite modern, employing the latest hygienic technology. My grandma's bakery and my uncle's were similar to all the old ones in Chelm . . . located in a basement, always filling up with water when it rained and difficult to keep clean (not that they did not try). I suppose the combination of moisture and heat brought insects to the place. My grandmother, who co-owned the bakery with her daughter, was a very strong woman. She never cared for my mother, so she decided that if my father really wanted to emigrate, he should sell his bakery to his family. At first my mother had no objections, but she had a premonition that if we sold out to the family, we would end up with nothing, because they had very little cash, and in order to emigrate, my parents needed funds. Her fears proved correct because when they started to negotiate, it was felt that my father should leave by himself, and my mother and I should remain in Chelm. We were to move out of our house, and let my father's mother, my uncle Yankel's and my aunt Havele's families occupy it, for which they would give us a stipulated sum of money so that my father would be able to emigrate.

My mother, who had been separated from her father during the First World War, and never got to see him after it was over, said she was not dividing her family. She insisted that we all leave together or else no one should go. My parents started looking for another buyer among the non-Jewish bakers. The man who was sharing the deliveries to the government-sponsored agencies with my father, and who was also a friend of his, offered us a substantial amount of cash for the bakery, the house, and for all the things we possessed. My paternal grandmother was gravely agitated that my father should even consider negotiating with that non-Jewish baker. She felt that he should sell to the family, even though she could not raise enough money.

As a result of this, as I later learned, my grandmother wrote to her son in Australia telling him not to send us the emigration papers. My uncle, faced with a dilemma, decided to send papers for all the Berlands. To be fair, he stopped working on our papers so that he might bring all the others up to the same level of completion. Both my grandmother and my father accepted this plan. We had no idea then that the resulting delay would cause the failure of our emigration.

Eventually my parents sold the bakery to my father's friend, the non-Jew, Mr. Granatovicz. It was 1938 and my parents were waiting for me to graduate from gimnazium because they did not want me to transfer in the middle of the year. I graduated in June of 1938. In August of the same year we left for Warsaw with what was left of our worldly possessions.

We went there for a short stay, reasoning that, since our papers had been worked on for almost a year, they would arrive momentarily, and my uncle kept assuring us that most of the formalities were completed and that whatever was left would be finished soon.

Before we left for Warsaw, my mother found a suitable family who agreed to take in my mother's mother, give her a separate room and kitchen privileges, and give her the supervision and support she might require. Financial provisions to assure her independence and comfort were put in place.

We were reunited with grandmother after we returned from Warsaw. She was still living with the same family, and assured us that they took good care of her.

A short time after we returned to Chelm, grandmother contracted typhus and died soon thereafter. Grandmother was in her early sixties at the time.

We moved in with my mother's cousin Rosie in Warsaw. She too had an only child and they all lived in a rather small apartment. We knew it was an inconvenience for the family because my aunt and uncle (I call them aunt and uncle) moved everything including their daughter into their bedroom, which was huge. A bed for my mother and father was placed in the dining room, which was rather small—the bed opened at night, we had to move the table—and I slept on a small cot in the entrance hall. We retired late and had to rise early so that the house would be ready for our relatives to enter. My aunt's brother, who was well-off and lived in a much larger apartment on another street, suggested that we stay with him, but we decided not to move since we were all expecting to leave for Australia very soon.

My mother watched over the expenditures very zealously. After we sold the house my mother became the cashier, supervising all the money they received from the sale. My father couldn't tolerate the fact that she doled out spending money to him. Weeks passed into months and my father could not "hang" around doing nothing. He knew many people in Warsaw and he secured a job as a supervisor. He would now have his own money. He and I were in cahoots because he didn't tell mother how much money he earned and when he and I went for a walk, he would give me some extra cash and ask me not to tell my mother that he had the additional money.

Eventually he became restless. It was already winter and we were still living there. It was not only uncomfortable for us, but for my aunt and uncle as well. One cold, brisk December day, my father and I went to the main post office, and we placed a transoceanic call to my uncle. Again he decided not to tell my mother about this. I will never forget that day. He had to enter a small telephone booth through a mahogany door. I can still see it. It was not large; my father went inside and I remained outside. He was talking with my uncle in Australia. He spoke very loudly. Then I heard my father repeat, "No! No! No!" Australia had closed the quota! It was thus impossible for anyone to emigrate.

I later learned that my uncle had never completed the processing of our papers at grandmother's insistence because she was angry at my father for having sold the bakery and the building to a *goy*[6] and therefore deprived his family of much needed income.

My father was terribly upset. He was already despondent about the sale of his business. He subsequently sought out some of his friends who had proper connections. From them he learned that the only place we could emigrate to at that time was Bolivia. But in order to go there, funds were required. The total amount needed was about three thousand dollars per person. That covered the properly completed papers and the cost of transportation to Bolivia.

After my father found his way out of the uncomfortable situation that necessitated his dependence on others, he came home feeling cheerful. He told my mother that we had a solution that wouldn't entail our imposition on others. We had to leave together. We just wouldn't have much cash to take with us. My mother was adamantly opposed. She suggested that perhaps he would go by himself and we would follow. He reminded her that she had once objected to separating us. Now suddenly, when it came to spending the money, she was reneging. Her argument was that at that time in Poland, in 1938, ten thousand dollars was a great sum of money for people in our circumstances and that it was not wise to spend it all because they had worked very strenuously to accumulate it.

Well, the entire family got together and talked about it, and my father went back to the Bolivian Consulate for more information. He was told that if he left immediately with cash, opened a bakery, and established himself as a financially independent person who could contribute to the Bolivian economy, he could request papers for us very soon thereafter. This was the beginning of April. My father was assured that by June all the paperwork would be ready and we could get our exit visas almost immediately.

This placated my father a little. He didn't object too much that I sided with my mother, which my father believed was always the case when there was an issue between my mother and him. I was not too enthusiastic about going to La Paz because I would, of necessity, have to learn a new language. So, the decision was that my father would leave alone and we would join him soon thereafter.

---

6. Non-Jew

Chapter 2

THE PRE-GHETTO ERA IN WARSAW

WHILE WE WERE IN WARSAW, Jewish refugees from Germany started returning to Poland. They had lost all their possessions in Germany. Many were Polish citizens who had moved to Germany and who had become economically self-sufficient there. They were sent to the Polish border. Poland didn't want them, but they finally did enter Poland after a great deal of difficulty.

Shortly after I arrived in Warsaw, I started to study English at a Berlitz school that met in a Jewish Y. Suddenly there was a shortage of rooms and we were able to see, when we came in for classes, that army blankets were being used to partition the large rooms. There were army cots behind the blanket dividers, with people living out of whatever little bundles they had; these were the refugees from Germany. We listened to them with excitement and trepidation, but we really didn't absorb too much. I remember coming back home and telling my family about what I had seen and heard. My uncle Hershel, who was really skeptical said, "Well, they were Polish and why did they have to go to Germany?" We kept telling him, "It is not just the Polish Jews; they are informing us that the German Jews are having trouble as well." My uncle couldn't be convinced. He was sure that the Polish government was democratic and that it could never happen in our country. But, in the meantime, my father was saying, "Look at what happened to me. It was done in an oblique sort of way, not very direct, but nevertheless it did happen to us."

None of this made an impression on my mother whose only concern was about all the money she could save if we did not leave together. And even with the example of the past experiences with her own father, she still paid no attention.

My father's papers were completed by the middle of April, but he decided not to leave until after the Passover seders. Passover was celebrated on the 21st and 22nd of April, and after the second seder the entire family got into taxis and brought my father to the main railroad station in Warsaw. There he boarded a train to travel to Gdynia, the only Polish port, to board a boat to Bolivia. He left, and whatever had been planned, he accomplished. He opened a bakery in La Paz the first week after he arrived there, and sent us papers soon thereafter.

Soon after my father left for Bolivia, my mother decided that she did not want to stay in our cramped quarters. She was tired of having to put up with my aunt's activities. My aunt was involved in extramarital activities with a medical doctor active in the army. She met with him regularly and one day he told her that he was on alert and on 24-hour duty. She was absolutely beside herself when she heard his news. That's how we knew, in our household, that something drastic was imminent. Although she was very cagey in telling my uncle how she knew, her attachment to this man was like a top military secret that everybody knew. My uncle was very religious and he did not go to the movies or the theater. When he had a day off, he would go to the *bes Midrash*[7] to study the Talmud, and it was then that she would go off on her little sprees, saying that she was going to the movies with my mother.

I recall the day my uncle came home and found her fainting and asking for smelling salts, and my uncle wondered "Why are you so upset? They are not going to take me; your father and your brother are too old to go. There are no sons in the family. Why are you so worried?"

My mother felt obliged to pretend that she was going to the movies with my aunt, this for my uncle's benefit, and my aunt would leave my mother to go to her assignation with her lover. Sometimes it rained, and my mother was bored with seeing the same movie again and again. We all liked our uncle; he was a lovely, kind person and my mother was tired of her role as alibi-provider. Mother decided that we would move and if my aunt wanted to say that she was going to visit my mother, then at least my mother didn't have to lie. So we rented a room for ourselves in another area, though not too far.

In June we received our visas for Bolivia. Getting boat passage for the trip presented a problem. Finally my father was able to get us accommodations for September the fifth of 1939. We had all our luggage stored in the central station a week in advance to be delivered to Gdynia and forwarded to the boat. We were supposed to leave Warsaw on the second or the third of September. The family tendered us farewell parties, but we already knew that the news was grim. Towards the end of August, there was a general mobilization. There was a great deal of unrest in the streets; one could feel the tension. People were expecting something drastic to happen. We would go to the American and English Consulates, where we heard promises of aid by representatives of both countries.

---

7. Prayer and study house

The general world situation was becoming very tense. One day in August my aunt visited and said that war was inevitable. In such situations families should be together, and my aunt insisted that we move back. So we moved back with them. My uncle was a secretary in a yeshiva. He also managed huge buildings in Warsaw. He got that job through his wife, because at one point she had an affair with a man who owned a large apartment house. Once this landlord gave my aunt a beautiful and expensive gift. My uncle believed that the landlord gave it to her in appreciation of his work since he would not accept a gift for himself. My uncle barely made a living, but for him it was enough.

I later learned that their daughter, who was my age (eighteen years), knew that her mother was dating other men and was absolutely heartbroken about it. On the last day of August, just before the war erupted, my uncle decided that all the monies he had collected for rent shouldn't be in his house. So he enlisted me and my cousin, Genia, to go to the bank to deposit the money. Then my uncle would be sure the landlord would have the rent payments. God forbid that my uncle should have it in his possession if there was a war. He didn't have a penny to his name but he would not take what was not his. He also had a direct line to God — that's how he knew that the war would not come to Warsaw. I remember, that day, going down the street towards the bank with my cousin. She was taller than I. Suddenly she grabbed my hand and shoved me into a building. She didn't let me look out but I was very curious. All these structures had big heavy, wooden gates, with little peep holes in them. When she turned around, I looked through an opening. It seems that she had seen her mother with this military man of hers walking arm in arm. Genia didn't want me to see them, but I knew from some of the things my mother had said that my aunt was not a devoted wife. I said to Genia, "I saw them." She broke down and spoke to me about how much she had to bear silently because she loved her father and didn't want him to know. Knowing what I know now, I believe my uncle must have known all along because it would have been impossible to keep the secret all through these years.

When we returned from the bank my aunt was already home with her smelling salts.

Chapter 3

GERMANY INVADES POLAND

THE WAR STARTED on September first, soon after we moved back with our family, and our plans to emigrate were useless.

We woke up to a distant yet persistent roar of engines. As the noise came closer, we recognized the sound as that of low flying airplanes, and before we realized how scared we were, other louder dins drowned out the roaring. This time we heard a series of tremendous explosions coming in quick succession. We realized that the Germans were bombing Warsaw, and we were paralyzed with fear. We all ran to the shelter in the front building.

We were told not to venture out of the building to watch. I remember running down the stairs and into the courtyard separating our building from the front one where the shelter was located. In the process I literally bumped into a young fellow who was evidently hit by shrapnel. He was running and screaming because he was obviously in pain; as I moved toward him I accidently touched him. I felt something wet, slippery, and warm. I later learned that I had felt the inside of his belly that was ripped open. I was immobilized, I couldn't move, I couldn't speak. Luckily, my mother was right behind me and she grabbed me and pulled me away. We were able to remain in our building for a couple of days. During the following days, our neighborhood, like all the others, was bombed twice or three times daily.

It is important to note that the Germans bombed Warsaw methodically and accurately. They targeted all bridges, utilities, crossroads, Jewish holy places, cemeteries, and, most frequently, Jewish neighborhoods. Two kinds of bombs were used: those that demolished buildings and those that started fires.

Our living quarters were firebombed and we had to leave. In a way, we were prepared for evacuation. Each of us kept a small bundle of clothes which we felt were essential for survival. My uncle had a relative who lived nearby, and he thought it was a good idea for us to start for her house. After running through streets of burning houses covered with broken glass and debris, we arrived at the relative's house. The building was still intact and my uncle directed us upstairs. As we walked into the structure we were assailed by an overpowering odor of ammonia. Somebody yelled, "This is gas!" Everybody panicked. We went out and asked fire marshalls for instructions. We were told to remain downstairs, and as we stood there, the bombers returned and dropped their missiles on buildings all around us. As we huddled, we heard a sudden shrill, piercing whistle, and felt a strong wind indicating that a bomb was being dropped on us. I was wearing a kerchief on my head and I always wore glasses. I immediately put my head down and placed my kerchief over my glasses so as to avoid getting glass slivers in my eyes. I was prepared for this bomb to smash us all. It landed on the building, but not exactly where we were. The structure shook, cracked, and large chunks of plaster started to fall on us. Suddenly, I found myself buried under a deluge of gravel. I felt something warm, but I didn't know what it was. There was a long silence. The bombers left and I didn't know whether I was dead or alive. I assumed that I was alive because I was thinking.

I was actually saved by a horse. When the bomb fell, a horse that belonged to the Polish Cavalry assigned to patrol the streets, was hit by a huge boulder. Fortunately, I fell very close to the horse, and was cushioned by its soft belly.

Then I heard people talking. My mother was calling me, "Where are you? Where are you?" I couldn't answer because the kerchief that I put over my head was covered with sandy material, small chunks of cement from bricks. I was afraid to move for fear that I would get dust in my eyes and/or in my mouth. Somebody grabbed me under my arms and slowly dragged me out. It was my mother, and as she pulled me out, my shoes kept slipping off my feet. I told her to stop and tried to grab hold of my shoes because I remembered that the streets through which we had walked were coated with cracked glass and I knew that I wouldn't be able to walk barefoot. I was wearing high-heeled shoes at the time because I was always self-conscious about being short. After I grabbed the shoes and my mother succeeded in getting me out, we looked for our relatives. We found our aunt, uncle, and cousin. The rest of my family was on the other side of the horse. People helped each other. Those buried in the gravel tried to cooperate with the rescuers, except for my aunt who became hysterical. She screamed and complained. My uncle dragged her out and she lost her shoes. At first, she refused to get out of the ruins and move on.

We were all so happy to be alive that we started to run into the street. My aunt had nothing on her feet and she couldn't walk on the broken glass. My uncle was taller than she, but she was heavy. Even though he wanted to, he couldn't carry her. Her daughter and my uncle took her around their shoulders and helped her along. My uncle told us that his rabbi lived on that corner. He thought that if we got to the rabbi's house we would be safe. God would not allow a bomb to hit his home.

We were distraught when we reached the rabbi's home. I don't remember his name. He lived on the first floor in a back building. (In Europe, buildings have a front, a backyard and a courtyard, and the first floor is on the second level.) Not everybody was allowed to visit the rabbi. Since my uncle studied the Torah with the rabbi we were allowed to enter. Those who saw us enter were startled because we were covered with dust and rubble. Our hair was white and seemed to be electrified. My aunt was clutching a little pillow. She was a self-indulgent lady. Each of us carried overnight changes; she had a small pillow only because she could not sleep without it. When we walked into the room there was a gasp. Something that had once been alive and was now dead had stained the pillow. Apparently it was someone's brain.

The room was very long and was empty of furniture so that more people could fit in. They sat on chairs which were lined up against both long walls. There was a small passageway to another room containing lots of books and shelves. In the center of that room the rabbi stood in white stockinged feet, wearing a prayer shawl. He was praying; so were the people in the long room. We were offered seats because we looked as if we had been through hell.

We sat down and caught our breath. It was extremely quiet. Just then my aunt remembered what we have been through and became hysterical. My uncle tried to calm her. We sat there for a while, feeling somewhat reassured and strengthened by the rabbi's presence. Suddenly, the planes were overhead again. Everybody prayed and cried, and hoped that the bombs would not hit us. A bomb did fall on another part of the building. Everything in the room shook, but we weren't touched. The rabbi sent a message from his room that perhaps it was not safe, and that we should leave the building. Even though another part of the place was hit, it was still risky to stay; there was a distinct probability that this section of the building might crumble. While we sat, people became introspective and did not talk with each other, but when we started moving out, they pushed one on top of the other. It was impossible to move in any direction. People panicked.

After struggling to reach the door, we could not get downstairs because people were descending from the higher floors. Unlike us, everyone else carried huge valises. My cousin and I were outraged by the fact that people were so concerned with their possessions that they blocked the entrance to the staircase with their valises instead of letting other people go down. My cousin, my uncle, my mother, two young men, and I erected a sort of barricade on the stairs. We asked people to form a single file, which had the effect of making the crowd a little more orderly. People were crying, screaming, and fearful that they would not get out of the building before it collapsed.

We walked back to the street where we had lived, Ciepla. It was rather late and it was very quiet. We looked for a house which was still intact and finally found one at a corner. It was half a block from where we lived. My uncle knew the superintendent and asked permission for us to use their shelter. The tenants were opposed, but my uncle managed to arrange for us to use the cellar where we found a nook for our family in a corner. We remained there for the duration of the bombing. The house was shelled, but from deep in the cellar we didn't hear what was going on. We were aware of the bombing, but we were safe below ground. We were afraid that if the building were hit we would be buried alive, so someone stood watch at the entrance to the cellar.

I became very ill soon after we moved into the shelter. I was frightened, and developed a high fever. When it became a little calmer, my uncle stepped outside to assess the situation. He came back and told us that there was still some shelling taking place, but that the heavy bombing had stopped. He heard that there was talk of a possible cease-fire soon. We didn't take any chances and stayed in the cellar for a couple of days. I don't remember what we ate. Maybe the tenants shared their food with us. I didn't know what was happening around me. My mother tried to get whatever she could to sustain us.

My uncle was an administrator of buildings in an affluent section of Warsaw. Only a few rich Jews lived there. After the cease-fire he went there only to find that some of the residents had abandoned their apartments and allegedly fled Poland because they had advance knowledge about the war. Most of them were government officials and the rumor was that people with close connections in the government were forewarned and left Poland just before the war started. Some even said that a number of high Polish Government officials had left the country to form a government in-exile in England. As a result, many of the apartments in the most desirable sections of the city were vacant. As the administrator, my uncle was able to get an apartment for himself. He returned to the cellar with the joyful news that he had been assigned a marvelous apartment for his family.

My mother asked him, "What about us?" He said, "Well, I don't think that you would fit into that neighborhood because you seem too provincial and look Jewish." As sick as I was, I understood what he meant. I became so upset that my fever soared and I developed diarrhea. My mother did not know what to do with me. Most of the people had already left the cellar. My mother and I were the last ones left. She was terribly distressed.

She tried to make me comfortable. She went to the apartment in which we lived after my father left for Bolivia. The first floor and the parterre were still intact although the second and third stories were bombed out. To accommodate everyone, people who lived on the lower floors made room for those who had occupied the upper ones. The landlady told my mother that her entire apartment was occupied. There was a family living in the living room, another in the room which we had used, and she shared a bedroom with her husband and two daughters. When my mother told her our story, she insisted that we stay with her. I think that I had dysentery, but no one considered the possibility that I might infect them. The bathrooms were destroyed. I had a pot in the corner and a small bed in which I slept with my mother.

We remained there for about two weeks until my mother was able to reach my uncle Moshe, the brother of the aunt with whom we had lived. He resided further from the center of town in a large apartment which he offered to share with us. When we moved in with that uncle on Chlodna Street, we had our own room. The situation became a little easier for me and my mother, and so I felt better.

At this point I would like to summarize what had happened in Poland.

At dawn on September 1, 1939, Hitler's air force, followed by other branches of the German army, launched a surprise attack on Poland, with whom Germany seemingly had friendly relations up to this point. Encountering little or no opposition from the Polish army, the Nazi military succeeded in conquering Poland and moving east, incorporating large parts of northern and western Poland into Germany.

At exactly the same time, Stalin, with whom Hitler signed a non-aggression pact shortly before the outbreak of hostilities, ordered his army to move into Poland from the east. Following some military engagements, the Polish army was forced to surrender and the Soviet Union took over the remaining southern and eastern parts of Poland. Initially, Chelm was occupied by the Soviet Union, but sometime in November 1939, when the borders between Russia and Germany were finalized, and the river Bug became part of the natural border, the Russians moved out of Chelm.

As soon as they settled into their newly acquired territories, the Nazis began instituting their anti-Jewish policies.

As their first move, they ordered the Jews in every city to form a self-governing body, which was called *Judenrat*.[8] It was supposed to be an elected body, but few

---

8. Council of Jewish elders

Jews wanted the job, so the Germans had to appoint some members arbitrarily. The Judenrat was charged with implementing all orders given by the Gestapo. This was not always easy, so the Judenrat created a Jewish police force to help them administer the orders and to maintain order.

The next point of order was to make the Jewish population easily identifiable and accessible. For this purpose, all Jews were ordered to wear specifically designated markings on their outer garments when they were outside their own homes. In some areas, Jews were required to wear a yellow Star of David on their chests, and on their backs. In other areas, the Jews were ordered to wear a white armband with a blue Star of David on their left arms. In Chelm and in Warsaw, I wore a white armband. One was severely punished if caught without the designated mark.

The Jewish-owned stores also had to display a clearly visible sign stating that they were Jewish enterprises.

All Jews were ordered to divest themselves of all movable and immovable possessions. Land and buildings were confiscated by the Germans immediately. Gold, silver, furs, leather, Persian rugs, valuable paintings and art pieces, antiques, silverware, good china, and crystal had to be delivered to a specifically designated place.

Jewish children were not allowed to go to school. Jewish professionals were fired from their jobs, and, at best, could only work for other Jews.

In 1941, Jews were ordered to move into ghettos that were usually located in the oldest and most dilapidated sections of the town or the city. Some ghettos were fenced in; others were not. The Warsaw ghetto had a wall; Cracow had barbed wire. The Chelm ghetto was open, but Jews were forbidden to be outside the designated area. When the ghettos were set up, a curfew was imposed on the Jews: seven p.m. in the summer, and earlier in the winter.

Food ration tickets for Jews were issued prior to the establishment of the ghettos.

In the beginning of 1942, the SS men started grabbing Jews from the street at random. They wanted them as laborers locally, or for resettlement to other places, which meant transports to concentration camps. This form of random grabbing was soon refined to regular and official requests for a specified number of Jews to be delivered by the Judenrat to a designated collection place. Though the Germans did not have to account for their actions, their requests for a contingent of people usually stated that workers were needed inside Germany.

Between the end of 1942 and some time in 1943, the Nazis liquidated all Jewish ghettos, thus making Poland Judenrein. In liquidation, the Jews were shipped to concentration and extermination camps.

Chelm was officially liquidated on November 6, 1942, and Cracow on March 13, 1943. I was part of both liquidations.

Uncle Moshe lived with his two sons, his wife, and his mother-in-law. They occupied a large apartment in a huge dwelling with two courtyards. While we stayed with them the building became self-governing. Those who were still able-bodied, worked. My mother tried to help out. She went outside of Warsaw to buy potatoes, tomatoes, and whatever else was available. It was a long walk to reach the outskirts of Warsaw, but she managed it somehow. Her desire to keep us alive gave her the strength to carry on. After a while, she went out into the Polish community to sell some of the things that the Jews who couldn't work and needed money had to sell in order to buy food.

I was drafted by the house committee to teach in the building because Hitler forbade Jewish children to attend school. I also found tutoring jobs on the outside and that is how I earned money. What I thought was a great idea was the organization of a little kindergarten, a babysitting program, and the sharing of various classes. Anyone with talent was drafted to keep the children occupied and studying. Select young people were sent to the well-to-do families to ask for food leftovers, and even to ask that they cook a little extra so we could have sustenance for the needy in our complex. As a young person, I was fascinated by the resourcefulness of some of the housekeepers. Once someone showed me that she was cooking tiny red radishes for dinner. She was stewing them with a few onions. Some were fortunate enough to have meat, but we, the collectors, could never get any; the only food we were able to get was the extra bread and vegetables that some people could spare. We had no kitchen in which to cook, but we did have a room from which we dispensed the food. We also distributed clothing for the children and for those who had nothing to wear.

The teaching, the food collecting, and other activities were very worthwhile. Every evening we met to devise methods of helping each other. We also discussed politics and other topics of the day. We were teenagers, so we had fun and flirted. My mother decided this was no way to live. She started to think about returning to Chelm, and she reached out to make contact with someone there.

In the meantime, rumors persisted that the Germans were going to form a ghetto. One of my students lived near the location where they decided to build the ghetto wall, and I watched the work progress. The procedure for obtaining an apartment in the ghetto was quite complicated. One needed a connection. My uncle who owned a lumberyard (though it was taken away from him) was fairly well-off and was able to maneuver. He told us that he was not going to wait until the Judenrat assigned an apartment to him. He would find a place even if he had to pay for it. My mother and I understood that he might not be able to get a place for us. The message was clear; if we stayed we would have to wait for an assignment. We felt that since we had no connections, we could probably get a bed in someone's home without an opportunity to choose compatible people. My mother became more aggressive in her attempt to move back to Chelm. She contacted Mrs. Dzwigaj who had been a neighbor of ours there. She had some dealing with her even in Warsaw when she sold various articles. When this woman returned to Warsaw, my mother asked her to consider taking us back to Chelm.

Chapter 4

THE CHELM GHETTO

AT THE TIME, Jews were not allowed to travel by train. We had to remove our white armbands with the blue Star of David that distinguished us from the Poles. Mrs. Dzwigaj wanted to take a train that left Warsaw late in the evening and to travel at night. She purchased three train tickets and we boarded the train. I had no problems posing as a Pole, and my mother, dressed like a peasant in a big plaid shawl, looked like the other lady. We were petrified. Anyone who entered the car or spoke at all filled us with absolute and total fear. I feigned sleep as did my mother. It was a long ride on a slow train. Every so often Germans would come in, yell and push everyone around. The car was almost as huge as the one used for cattle. We were riding in third class where everybody was literally piled on top of each other. More seats than were actually available were sold, so it was extremely cramped. Fortunately, we arrived in Chelm before dawn. We went to our relatives, my father's sister, who had remained in her home.

In September 1939, when Hitler and the Soviets signed a non-aggression pact, the Russians took over Chelm. After a few weeks, Germany drew a new border that excluded Chelm from Russian territory.

Prior to moving out, the Russians invited some of the Jewish people to migrate to Russia. They said, "Why would you want to stay with the Germans? You know what is happening." They offered trucks and accommodations. But people refused to believe the horror stories. They didn't want to surrender their homes, possessions and businesses. Few accepted the Russian offer.

Soon after the Germans moved into Chelm, they summoned all the prominent Jews to the central town square. They ordered them to march toward the Russian border on the pretext that they were to be deported to Russia. This happened on December 1, 1939, and was in fact the very first official action against Jews. I have been told that these important people were surrounded by armed soldiers and their dogs, and the Jews were marched briskly to the river Bug.

They were moved quickly and those who were not able to keep up the pace were shot on the spot. That is how my father's oldest brother Yankel Berland died.

My father's oldest sister's husband, Sroel Lis, was wounded. He rolled into a ditch, played dead, and the marchers moved on. After they passed, some peasants took my uncle to their house. They called our family who came for him. When he returned, doctors were still living in the city, and he was nursed back to health.

In Chelm, mother and I moved in with my father's younger sister. My aunt Sara lived in a private home in a section of the town where few Jewish families resided. Shortly after the march her husband and son moved to the eastern part of Poland, which was then occupied by Russia. The Russians vigorously encouraged Jews to leave territories occupied by Hitler. Unfortunately, the small towns occupied by the Russians could not accommodate all of these refugees. Overcrowding made it necessary for people to sleep in hallways and on the streets. Too many fled from small towns like Chelm. The Russians decided to allow volunteers to register for work inside Russia. Those who wished to return to their German-occupied home-towns could apply for permission.

However, when the Jews who chose to return to German-occupied Poland learned that they had been loaded onto trains bound for Siberia, the Russians reportedly explained, "If you are a Jew and you are aware of what is going on in Germany, and you still wish to return to Germany, you must be an enemy of Russia." Thus, as punishment, they were shipped to Siberia. Those who were physically able to withstand the terrible weather and arduous working conditions, survived the war. Most who went back to German-occupied Poland did not.

One of my uncles who wanted to return to Chelm was sent to Siberia with his son. He survived, but his son did not. My other uncle, the husband of the aunt with whom we stayed, died along with his son. Other people from our town who were sent to Siberia survived.

Mother and I stayed with my aunt for a few months. Then the Germans decided to move all Jews into one area, thus designating that section as a ghetto. It was not walled, there were no barbed wires or fences, but we were only allowed to live on certain streets in the most dilapidated part of town. One of the thoroughfares was called the Palestine Street. Many of the poor Jewish workmen like shoemakers and tradespeople lived there. My mother tried to contact some old acquaintances whom we had helped before the war. Using their influence, she succeeded in finding a suitable residence in the home of a family with whom we felt we could get along.

I was drafted by the Judenrat to work for the *Gemeinde*.[9] Since I was a gim-

---

9. Municipality

nazium graduate, I was expected to perform community chores, mainly among the poor, distributing tickets for bread rations. The difficult part about distributing the ration tickets was that the people who were entitled to them used to be afraid to come to the main office where they were previously to be had. Some people feared authority in general. Others were afraid that if they came to the Judenrat, they would be drafted for all kinds of jobs, and that's how the idea of going into the homes of various people originated. It started before we were all herded into the ghetto. What I found rather astonishing was that the women who allowed us to use their homes were poor ladies who lived in one room—or perhaps one with a small alcove, and with large families. When I walked into any of these quarters they were spotlessly clean as though for the Sabbath. The floors were scrubbed. All extraneous articles were put out of the way so that people could enter. Sometimes, if I arrived early and the woman was washing the floor, I would tell her that a great many people would be coming and that it really wasn't that important for her to expend so much energy scrubbing that floor. But she felt that it was a major contribution that she was making in allowing her house to be used as an office, so she wanted it properly clean.

One of the problems that arose at first was that people feared accepting their ration tickets. They knew that I was Jewish, but I represented the government and they were wary of me also. It took a long time for them to thaw out, and they were at times able to discuss some of their problems with me. At that time I didn't know much about the psychological aspects of the human condition. But I could empathize with some of the fears they exhibited. There was a great deal of sickness in these large poor families and a member would sometimes die during the week. Since we distributed a ticket to everyone in the family it became necessary to notify the authorities of the death. Yet, everyone could use the extra bread ration.

An ethical dilemma presented itself: what do you do if a family member died? Do you curtail the extra ration of bread? Some would report a loss and leave the decision to me; others would not, and see for how long they could get away with it. Unfortunately, there were some who knew that a neighbor had died, a son, or a mother, and they would appear in line behind a surviving family member to watch whether they imparted this news to me. If they didn't, these eavesdroppers would loiter until everyone left and would tell me, "Know what? So and so's grandmother died last week. They're cheating you." That's when I found myself in a very precarious situation. The only thing I could say to them was that this week's rations had already been allocated and if I did return this week's tickets, no one would be able to use them. It was a big risk, but in the end no one complained about me to the authorities.

The distribution of the tickets took me off the work list because, though there was not a regular labor force established as yet, the German procedure was to come into a neighborhood and seize anyone—either to sweep the streets or to clean their offices, or to do some other chores. So I did not have to do that. There was also some work that was done around our town that wasn't really necessary but was part of the psychological torture that the Germans imposed on people. There were meadows around the city that were wet. Some Jews were selected to dry these marshes; they might be apprehended, in the street or at home, and assigned to this, or a similar job. Jews were also used for jobs on the railroads, paving streets, digging ditches, and the like.

The choice chores were in the Gestapo offices or in the gardens that surrounded them. They were "plums" because then you were close to the authority, and sometimes, just by observing what was going on in the office, people could predict what would probably occur. Some worked in the office. They engaged a number of Jews as typists and office assistants. Office workers would get word of some of the forthcoming orders. Everyone was curious about when the Germans would come out and select people, or how many people they needed for work details, or where the jobs were available or when they would come to seize a contingent of people to send into the surrounding concentration camps.

I had two friends: one was a girl who was the daughter of our physician, Dr. Ochs. He was killed on the first march, and she worked in the gardens. I also knew a young man who had lived in the same neighborhood that I did when I was a child, and who now resided in the same building when we moved into the ghetto. Now he worked inside a Gestapo office. There was a great deal of talk among the people in the ghetto that he was a collaborator. I did not believe it chiefly because I was too close to him. He was older than I. Before the war, I wouldn't even have given him the time of day because he didn't attend gimnazium. But now, during wartime, with very few men available, any young man who complimented us was considered a good prospect.

In any event, this young man and his family lived on the ground floor of the building in which my mother and I lived on the first floor. We shared a room with our landlady, her son, and her daughter. My mother and I shared a bed and the woman who owned the apartment slept in another bed with her daughter, while her son used the sofa. There also was a bedroom, which was occupied by a family that consisted of four brothers and four sisters. This room contained wall-to-wall beds, and there was also a kitchen in which a young woman and her baby slept. Luckily, the people were kind, intelligent, and more or less compatible, so that we were able to work out a schedule for using the kitchen, cleaning, and other chores. Everybody left for work early each morning, and adhering to a time schedule helped. The brothers and sisters owned a large appliance store. This business was taken away from them, and since they sold electronics, they were able to obtain a job in their field.

We usually followed a rotating schedule for cooking. Everybody was responsible for cleaning his or her room, but the kitchen had to be done on a rotating basis. Naturally everybody had to clean up after cooking, but the floor had to be washed often and by each one because the kitchen was the first room you entered when you entered the house. Our sleep-in living room was next and then the room occupied by the sisters and brothers.

Now, everybody used to watch the comings and going of my friend because he had access to information about planned selections and/or deportations. If he was seen coming in a little earlier, we knew that something was about to happen. We would look out of the window from upstairs and note that the families living on the ground floor would walk out one by one: first, the mother with a little package under her arm, followed by the father after a short interval, then the sister, and finally the other people who lived there. When we saw that, every one of us tried to find a place to go outside of the ghetto, usually to a Polish friend with whom we might have a standing arrangement.

As I mentioned before, our ghetto was not encircled by walls or fences. There were just streets that were designated for Jews only and areas in which Jews were not permitted, especially during the evenings. When some action was anticipated, my mother and I would also leave. We would remove our white armbands and go to the Aryan area. I would call on one family, and my mother would go to another one. For about a year, if you were not home when the Gestapo came to seize you for work or deportation to camps, you could return the next day, and no one asked where you were. Nobody questioned you about what happened yesterday. You were back and life resumed its normal dreary course.

Now, as for life in the ghetto: the young people tried to create their own entertainment. We weren't allowed to go into the streets after seven in the evening. We visited each other: we played games, we sang songs, or told stories, almost anything to amuse ourselves. We would talk about what happened during the day and how matters developed, and so on. I had very few peers in my immediate circle at the time because some left when the Russians did and others really stayed close to their families. The building that we lived in, one next to ours and a few of the other small houses shared one large connecting backyard. In the summertime we would go there.

This continued until November 1942 when we started to hear that there were plans to liquidate the ghetto and make Chelm Judenrein. Nobody knew when it was going to happen. Nobody really believed that it would occur.

With all those worries, social consciousness prevailed and people DID try to help each other to the best of their abilities. As we had done in Warsaw, we tried to organize some classes to tutor the younger children. There were not too many young children in our building. We also tried to learn something about recognizing the symptoms of various illnesses so that we might be helpful in this area. No doctor was available, but there was a kind of healer, one who attempted to treat all kinds of physical problems that arose at the time.

I remember that those people who worked at drying the swamps, which were located near the railroad tracks, would tell us that trains filled with people traveled in both directions. They didn't really see the people, but they heard the screams. So we all prepared for the worst, anticipating the worst.

One time before we moved to the ghetto, the Germans were searching through the town to seize Jews. My father's oldest sister had three girls. One was my age and two were younger. At that time they were already living in the ghetto area. One day the Germans told the Judenrat that they needed a couple of hundred people to be delivered to the central square for "resettlement." This was an order that we all dreaded. I was still living with my Aunt Sara (shortly after I arrived from Warsaw). This was an Aryan neighborhood, therefore a bit immune from German searches.

In the middle of the night I heard a knock on the door and I was scared. I opened it and saw my cousin Toby. She said that something awful was happening in her neighborhood, and that the Germans had taken her parents and her sisters. Somehow, she had managed to run away and decided to come here because we were very close to a forest. It was late at night, she was very tired and very frightened and came into my bed. We had never been very close because our parents weren't. Her mother and mine didn't get along. It was the first time that we really spent hours talking about ourselves, our differences and similarities, and mostly how our hopes and fears were exactly the same. We heard shots and screams coming from a great distance.

When daylight arrived, she was afraid to stay. She said that eventually we would have to move, and she decided to hide elsewhere, either in the forest or where she believed that groups of partisans were gathering. I felt very strongly about her not leaving, I asked her to stay with us. She had seen her parents being taken away and she felt that there was no point in her remaining and continuing to live in Chelm. We embraced and kissed, and she quietly left our house and moved to the outskirts of town. She insisted that was it! It was the end! I said it couldn't be, because if we were still allowed to live outside of the ghetto, it could not be the end. There were other families still scattered all over town. Logic convinced me that they would herd us together. She left, and I never saw her again.

On the next day, we learned that my aunt, uncle, and the other two girls had been able to run away and hide. They were devastated when they found that Toby, their oldest daughter, had not wanted to remain with us. Of course, for a while they blamed me and my mother because we didn't insist urgently enough that she stay.

The Germans made selections of Jews often and with no specific regularity. During that routine, people were herded together. The SS[10] men chose whom they wanted in advance: first they decided to eliminate young children, then the elderly, the sick, those over forty, and so on. Eventually, we learned about the plan to rid the town of all Jews. A few days before this dreadful event, the young man who worked in the Gestapo (some said for the Gestapo) came to our room and hung around for many hours. My mother was despondent that I allowed him to do so. Maybe I shouldn't have. Perhaps I didn't want to know. I pretended. I had to believe that he was not a collaborator. Everybody else insisted that he was, and my mother and I had a great many arguments about that possibility, and why I permitted him to stay around the house or why I associated with him.

The day he came up to our apartment he said "You know, it looks like the Germans are preparing to clear out the town very soon." Nothing happened for a couple of days and then one afternoon we noticed that the young man's family left their home in single file, "like geese in a row," one after the other. That's how it appeared from our window. First the father, then the mother, the two sisters and after them, the other occupants of their apartments. They moved slowly, but surely. My mother and I quickly conferred. We decided where I would go and where she would. Before nightfall we slipped out through the back courtyard, just before the curfew. I crossed the street, removed my white armband, and left for the home of the people who lived in my aunt's neighborhood, Mr. and Mrs. Dzwigaj. Mrs. Dzwigaj was the woman who had brought us back from Warsaw.

I knocked on the door, but she was not at home. Her husband, Mr. Dzwigaj, and her daughter Maria were there. He was very angry that I came to them. He insisted that it was dangerous for himself and his family. I said "Look, I cannot get out now and, you know, I have been here several times before. It will probably quiet down tomorrow and I'll go home then." I hoped everything would be all right in the morning. Well, the next morning, he rose very early, went to work and in fifteen minutes he was back in the house screaming his head off. He in-

---

10. SS, or Schutzstaffel were the blackshirts, the elite guard of the Nazis. The term SS is used loosely to categorize any German, any Nazi, any Gestapo member with the most hateful designation that we could summon.

sisted that I get out. I asked him what happened and he said that posters were plastered all over town announcing that all the Jews in town would have to be deported. Any Aryan who was found harboring a Jew was subject to shooting and, if lucky, to imprisonment. In addition, the culprit's entire family would also suffer. He continued to yell and his daughter stood there, watching me. I thought that this was the end.

He dragged me to the window to show me how people were being herded on the street from everywhere with Polish policemen and German SS men clubbing them over the head, pushing and cursing the victims. I pleaded with him for time, but he was adamant.

Finally, Maria, who was my age, pitied me and said "You know if mother were here, she wouldn't throw her out."

"Well, mother is not here and I'm not assuming the responsibility, I really don't owe her anything. She's not such a close friend of mine for me to risk my life to save hers."

For the first time I was compelled to use all my faculties and resources to be logical in order to convince him. I said, "Look, they're clearing the town of Jews and they'll probably manage to complete the job during the day. It won't take them longer. You and Maria are going to work. If you lock the door from the outside and leave me in the house during the day, I'll draw the curtains and stay out of sight. I promise to leave in the evening, when it is dark and no one can see me."

I had lived in the ghetto for about two years.

Chapter 5

ESCAPE FROM CHELM

DURING THE DAY I thought a great deal about what I could do. I peeked out of the window from behind the curtains. I was transfixed, watching poor souls being prodded by rifle butts in the direction of the railroad station. I saw friends among them; I heard shots every so often. All the time I was thinking of what to do. Most of all, I was praying that Mrs. Dzwigaj should come back. I hoped that if she did she would direct me to another Polish family out of town who would hide me. She had a sister in Cracow or near there. I thought that she would really do that for me. I had been warned by Mr. Dzwigaj and by Maria that I should be very quiet. Their house did not have running water, so they left me a pail-full for the whole day. They warned me again to be quiet, so that the neighbors should not hear me or see me. If they saw somebody, they would report it to the authorities because there was a reward for such information: for bringing in a Jew one could receive a loaf of bread, because one would be turning in a traitor.

Well, the day passed. Mrs. Dzwigaj did not come home. Her husband did so, for supper—furious. The daughter came first, and she was crying. I guessed that she had bad news for me. She gave me a blow-by-blow description of what was happening in the city: and how they were dragging everyone out of the Polish houses, how all the Jews who were found were shot on the spot. She swore that she saw my mother being killed. I asked if she was sure. She told me where they dragged her out, and I knew that this wasn't the neighborhood in which my mother had planned to be. My mother had planned to go to a brand new area that they were building for railroad employees who were being relocated from Bydgoszcz to Chelm. (They were expanding the railroad system.) I thought she wasn't where Maria had mentioned, but I wasn't sure.

Once she told me that my mother had been shot, all my energy was sapped and I felt that there was nothing I could do any more. When Mr. Dzwigaj came home he angrily ordered me to leave at once. I had a difficult time pleading with him to wait until it got dark.

He said, "I don't care what you do and I'm not interested in where you go. Just go!"

Then Maria asked, "Where are you going? No one will take you in."

They were sure about that. At that time I felt that since my mother was dead, I had nothing to live for, I had no hope. I felt hemmed in, defeated! I believed that I had no way out. I was determined that I would not let the Germans take me alive, pack me into one of those cattle cars and drive me into a gas chamber. I wanted to end it all myself. I decided that the railroad tracks were a possible means for suicide.

Having been impressed by Tolstoy's *Anna Karenina,* who ended her life under a railroad car of an oncoming train, I decided to adopt this method. The railroad ran through the outskirts of the city. Chelm didn't have a tall building from which to jump. As I was growing up, I heard many stories about hopeless people who attempted to kill themselves by leaping in front of a speeding train.

I felt pressure, but I washed and changed my clothes. I dressed in my very stylish light gray coat, which was made especially for me to wear on our projected trip to Bolivia and it was, of course, too light in weight for that time of year, but I wore a sweater and a jacket underneath and I felt all *farputzt*.[11] I was now a bleached blonde. The Germans seemed more tolerant of fair-haired people. If your nose was small and straight, if you looked neat, and if your hair was blonde and straight, the Germans as a rule would not bother you. In contrast the Poles had an uncanny talent for recognizing a Jew no matter how one looked.

I went out into the street and walked towards the main thoroughfare, carefully watching the German soldiers. (The Dzwigaj family lived on a side street.) I noticed that the German patrols were all over the place. They would walk in pairs and they looked into every nook. They also looked intently into everybody's eyes. As I walked down a narrow sidewalk, two Germans walked towards me. As they moved closer, I had to decide whether to obey the rule or not; the rule was that if a German approaches on the sidewalk, Jews must step off the curb to make room for him to pass. Compulsively, I wanted to comply, but then I recalled that I was not supposed to be a Jew. Since there was no room for the three of us, and I didn't want to step into the gutter, I walked between them! In doing so, I bumped into them and said "Excuse me. I am very sorry. . . . I was so absorbed in thinking about other matters." They said that I was "fresh," and allowed me to pass. Frankly I thought that the bumping might divert suspicion about my being Jewish.

I had a couple of other encounters with the Germans who patrolled the streets.

---

11. Dressed up

I walked straight, looking them directly in the eyes. I pretended that I was in a hurry, because the Poles also had a curfew, though a later one. All along I was rushing towards the railroad. The trains crossed the main street, and there were far fewer houses as I approached the railroad. I was thinking about my intent to commit suicide and wondered whether I would dare to do so. Now I was scared. There was no one around. It was rather dark. Who walks along railroad tracks at dusk, in an elegant gray coat wearing high heels and carrying a little leather briefcase? That's all I had. Visually the whole picture seemed incongruous. Anyone who might notice me would know that I was not a clerical person, nor an official.

I stopped thinking about these things. I kept going. I was at the end of my rope. I assumed that my mother was dead. I didn't have the strength to fight. I had no purpose in life; no strength to walk. I sat down at the bottom of the railroad embankment. I waited there between a couple of bushes, so as not to be seen, and I listened for the sounds of an oncoming train because when one comes from a far distance, the embankment usually quivers. I felt some movement. I went up on the tracks and lay face down between the rails. I stayed in that position for what seemed an eternity. I don't know how long it actually was. I tried to conceptualize the meaning of death. I felt quite relieved. I believed that this was going to be the end. I would not have to worry any longer. My head was down. Suddenly, I heard a movement. I felt something poking my back, and I jumped up as if someone from another world was asking for me. It was a Polish railroad inspector in full uniform. He was carrying one of those portable kerosene lamps, and he looked at me. Of course the first thing he asked was, what was I doing there.

I was absolutely dumbfounded. I couldn't speak, not a word. I couldn't make my voice audible. He immediately realized why I were there. He said "Yes, I know. You must be a Jewish girl trying to end it all." He continued, "There is no reason for it." He repeated, "There is no valid reason to die."

I argued, "What do you mean no reason? My mother was killed. I have nothing."

He countered "Look, you are young and you don't look especially Jewish. Your hair is blonde."

Anyhow, I told him I had no place to go, had no strength, and was utterly exhausted.

He then told me, "Not far from here, perhaps a couple of miles further down the tracks there's a little forest." He was sure that there were some partisans, young Jews, there. He suggested that I go there. He was certain they would take me in and would supply the support that I wanted and needed.

That's what I did. It was already dark then, as I walked towards the forest. I did not know exactly in which direction to move, but I eventually found the entrance.

As I approached the woods a man stopped me. He was a forester, and he said, "Hey, Jew, where are you going?"

I replied, "What do you mean Jew?"

He raised his voice belligerently, "Don't you kid me. I know you Jews run away like mice. I'm not going to let you into the forest. It is my responsibility to keep your kind out of here."

I engaged him in a long conversation; we spoke about patriotism and humanity. I eventually asked him, "What will you get for turning me in? You won't even receive a loaf of bread. I'm a human being. I will give you more than bread." I had a ring. It was a nice one. I gave it to him and he let me go.

He warned me, "You can't go back because the Germans will catch you."

I said, "Don't you worry about whether I can or can't go back. Just don't report me." He took my ring and left. He was sure that I would be caught sooner or later.

I went back to the railroad tracks about halfway from where I had started. I was entirely spent. I couldn't manage to place one foot in front of the other. As I inched along the embankment, I noticed a haystack just a few steps from the tracks. I thought that I would be able to sit down and rest. I dug a little hole in the hay and crawled in. I think I fell asleep before I even sat down. That's how weary and inert I felt. I don't know how much time elapsed. I suddenly felt something crawling near me, and I froze.

Before I realized what was happening, I was being seized by two huge hands. I had entered the haystack head first and my feet were therefore outside. I had to struggle to get out. I saw a huge silhouette of a human being; it was a man, a peasant who was stinking drunk. He knew immediately that the only person who would be hiding in a haystack at that time of the night would be a Jew. He called me a dirty Jewess. He offered to give me a fun time and babbled; "Hey, what do you have to lose," and "blah, blah, blah." He was so drunk and I was so terribly frightened and mad that as I moved out, I shoved him with such force that he rolled over and I don't think he had the strength to get up. He lay there blubbering under his breath. I sat quietly to see what his next move would be, but apparently he was too stoned to stand up. Before I realized it, he fell fast asleep and when that happened, I started running.

I didn't want to go in the direction of my encounter with the train inspector or to the other location of my meeting with the forester. I crossed the tracks and headed toward the other side of the embankment. I kept running. I came to a huge open space, with no buildings or forest, just meadows or fields which were empty at that time. It was night. As I was moving on, I noticed a barn which was only half completed. It had four walls and a roof, but was supported by four piles so that from the ground to the walls there was a space. Still, it was a structure with an enclosure and I decided to take shelter there. I walked in through the open part and in one corner I noticed some straw or hay, I don't remember which it was. That's where I lay down and decided to spend the rest of the night planning my future course of action.

I slept soundly and woke at dawn. I decided that I would not move during the day lest someone see me. I remained there through the day. Though hunger and the cold had not bothered me too much during my running, it was already about twelve hours later, I had left the city at about four o'clock in the afternoon and it was now the next morning at four o'clock, I really started to feel the hunger, the cold, the discomfort of my swollen feet, and I was afraid to remove my shoes because I knew that I would have difficulty in getting them back on. While I lay there during the day immobilized with fear and suffering from the cold and hunger, I decided that, when it got a little darker, I would walk into town to see whether I could hear some news and try to get something to eat. Maybe I could find out if Mrs. Dzwigaj had returned; perhaps if she were home, she might find a way for me to hide somewhere or, if possible, take me to some hideout. It was November; a light snow started to come down, and it was bitter cold.

Chapter 6

MORE CLOSE CALLS

IN THE DARK I returned to the city slowly; I don't remember meeting anyone, or going any place in particular, or even how I looked. I wasn't cold, and I hoped that I looked fairly decent. When I got back to the city I headed for the Dzwigaj family. Maria answered the door. She said that her mother had not returned yet, and that I had better "beat it" because if her father saw me, he would undoubtedly take me right to the German Collection Center. She also told me that the main firehouse had been converted into a central collection depot. Anyone picked up was brought there.

I told her, "I am very hungry, could you give me something to eat?"

She ran into the house and I heard her father ask, "Who is there?"

She answered, "Oh, the neighbor wanted to ask a question."

Perhaps he suspected that something was wrong, but he chose not to be too inquisitive. She brought me a buttered roll and a glass of some liquid. I don't remember what it was, but it was cold. I ate and drank and then walked out of the house, trying to be very careful because I knew that if the neighbors saw me, they would inform the authorities, not only against me, but they would involve my friends as well. I wasn't dead yet, and realized that I still might need them. I didn't want to endanger or harm them.

From there, I decided to walk crosstown to call on the people to whom we had sold our house and bakery. Since it was a secluded place, even though there were some little houses nearby, maybe there were people who might have heard or seen my mother. I don't know what I hoped to gain there, but I went. I entered through the backstairs and they recognized me at once. When the lady of the house saw me, she almost fainted. She asked me to please leave. But I told her that first of all I wanted to know whether my mother had come here. I surmised that if I had the idea to come here, she might also have had the same thought. She said, "Yes, she was here. She bathed and changed her clothes. Then she left when the shooting started and headed to another part of town."

When she asked about my hiding place, I broadly described the location of the lonely unfinished barn.

I told her that I needed a pair of shoes, a blanket, and something to place on my head. I was cold. She gave me a loaf of bread to take along because at that point I was not too hungry. She also brought me a warm drink and a huge woolen blanket, more like a bedspread than a blanket, but it was warm. She brought me a black felt hat that I put on and gave me her shoes and rubber overshoes. They were about three sizes too large but they were all right for me because my feet were badly swollen. I probably resembled a comic character and even in such a desperate situation I had to laugh when I looked at those huge galoshes on my feet. These people couldn't wait for me to leave. They asked me what I was planning to do, urgently advising, "Do whatever you have to—just get out of here."

I told them that I would need something to eat while hiding.

They said, "If you are careful and if you're not caught, we will give you some food when you come here next time, after dark. That is all you can expect from us."

To get to their house, actually the one that was once ours, a very roundabout route had to be used to avoid the firehouse. Going back now I felt a little more comfortable. Prior to this time, I walked very awkwardly with my swollen feet in those high heels, and now I fared a little better. As I moved down a street across from the firehouse, a young man stopped me and called me by my real name. It turned out to be a young man who had attended the same gimnazium that I had. He was in a class or two below me, but he was a big boy and now he recognized me. He started by saying, "What are you doing here? Don't you know that all the Jews have been sent away and those who are left are being rounded up? There is a collection point and you are not supposed to be in the street." I asked him to pretend that he did not see me.

He gave me a big spiel that he was a boy scout and that he must tell the truth. He had sworn to abide by the laws. I tried to talk him out of turning me over to the Germans, using some of my patriotic lessons that I had learned in school, that this is not the Germans' country and that he does not have the same obligations to them. He told me that in school the Germans had urged them to obey the laws. He said they had promised them all kinds of goodies and that they would receive a special award for every person they delivered into their hands. We stood there arguing for awhile and finally I had an idea that perhaps he could do both, turn me over, and retain his boy scout's honor and I could still try to run away.

A German soldier was marching back and forth from one end of the firehouse to the other, and I suggested that, to appease his conscience, he should bring me over to the firehouse at the time when the German was turning in the other direction. He would thereby be fulfilling his obligation as a scout and at that point I would take my chances. It took some time to convince him, but finally he said he would agree to my plan. We crossed the street together, and I walked very slowly, watching the soldier moving towards the end of the firehouse. The Germans have a very rhythmic manner of turning on their heel. And as the soldier turned, the young school boy went his way and I went off in the opposite direction. It happened right there in front of that firehouse! My heart pounded as I quickened my steps.

During my discussion with the young boy scout, I had worked on his feelings. Among other things I told him that when the Germans were finished with the Jews, they would most probably start persecuting Polish patriots who oppose the German rule of their country. I explained that the Germans would also attack all the teachers and the intelligentsia. Somehow I struck an emotionally valid and logical chord in him. Maybe it was luck. Once we started talking, my sincerity moved him. I reminded him that we had been schoolmates at one time and we shared the same high regard for our alma mater. Maybe this was why he let me go. With my blanket and my loaf of bread, I hurried back to the barn where I remained through the next day and part of the following night. All along the way I could hear the sound of scattered shooting and grenades exploding in the distance.

Covering myself with my warm blanket, I fell asleep with a heavy heart, but with my brain already seeking a way to do something constructive. Once again I decided to stay in the barn for the entire day and then in the evening I would return to the city where I would try to find my mother, who I was now convinced was alive.

As I lay there at dawn, I heard footsteps. I hid my entire body under the blanket. I heard a man's voice urging me to get up. It was the farmer who owned the barn. He immediately and angrily asked me what the hell I was doing there.

There was very little I could say in that situation. "You know what I am trying to do, I am trying to hide."

The farmer replied, "You can't stay here."

I said, "This barn is very far away from your home and until I can collect my wits and can devise a plan, I will not leave." I added that my mother was probably in hiding somewhere in the city, and as soon as I was able to find her, we would work out some plan. I asked him to please let me stay there.

He countered, "Don't you know that you are endangering me and my family?"

Again, I appealed to him and said "I am sure that you have young children, and wouldn't want the same thing to happen to them, so can't you let me stay at least until dark?"

He said, "Okay, but I want you out by the end of the day. Once you walk out of here, DON'T come back!"

I thanked him and about fifteen minutes later, he returned with a bottle of coffee and a piece of black bread and butter. He asked me whether I had eaten and I told him that I had gone into the city and received some bread. The farmer repeated: don't I know that each time I left the barn and came back I was endangering his entire family, and myself as well. He warned me not to walk out if there was snow on the ground, as footprints might give me away.

It was November. Poland is usually very cold during November. The farmer said, "I have little food for myself and I cannot bring you any more. The barn is not finished and my comings and goings to the place will raise suspicions. So make sure that you get the hell out of here. When you leave the next time, don't come back."

I told him, "In the meantime, you fed me and I have the bread, so there is no need for me to go to the city soon. If you will permit me to stay this one night, I will think of something else tomorrow."

He departed, after leaving the food. Later that evening I heard footsteps, and I thought, "Oh, my God he must have changed his mind, or maybe somebody else is coming." When I heard footsteps for the second time, I curled up in a fetal position, pulled the cover over my head, and thought, "All right, he'll come and he'll have to shoot me—I am not getting out from under this cover. I don't care. I don't have the strength to deal with this situation any longer."

The sound of footsteps stopped and I heard someone climbing into the barn. I tried to peek from under the blanket to see who was there. Suddenly, I heard my mother's voice very softly calling me by my name. I couldn't believe it.

I almost fainted, when I looked at her. Her face was black-and-blue. It seemed that she too had hidden in a haystack in a different section of the city. A couple of other Jews also hid in that place and some Polish children discovered them there. They went to bring the Germans who didn't bother to wait for the Jews to get out. They just shot into the haystack. Some of the people who were betrayed were killed, but my mother was just grazed by the bullets. Her forehead was bruised, and under her eye she was left with a black-and-blue mark. The bullet just missed her eye: it did not lodge in her body. It grazed the left side of her face, the cheek and the eye, and part of the forehead. I became so upset that I started to shake and cry. We hugged and kissed and we were at a loss to know how to react. She joined me on that little pile of hay under the blanket. Sitting there, we devised a plan. She was very tired so I suggested we try to sleep.

I was at a loss to understand how she learned where I was. There was no address here, no recorded mileage from the town. Then I remembered that when I was at the bakery and Mrs. Granatowicz gave me the blanket and as I was putting on the overshoes, she had asked where I was staying. I told her that I was hiding in an unfinished barn which was a couple of miles outside of town. Apparently on that day when I did not go to the city, my mother went there and this lady repeated what I told her. Thus, my mother found me in what seemed like the middle of nowhere.

Early the next morning, the peasant farmer came back and said: "Now there are two of you here and now I definitely want you both to leave."

Although he told us we had to go immediately, we persuaded him once again to allow us to stay until it was dark outside so that we could move undetected through the open field. When that time came, my mother and I moved out of the barn very cautiously. All we could see was dark sky and endless fields. We kept our fingers crossed as we walked on in no particular direction until we reached what looked like a small settlement. We headed directly toward a barn which was huge and completely finished. Since it was late now, we assumed that no one would be working in the barn. The doors were not tightly bolted so we sneaked through them. It was a tall structure comprised of several levels used for piling hay and straw. We started for a corner where we saw a ladder that reached up to just under the roof. Up there we hid in the straw and began to plan our next step.

I was very frightened entering that barn and I was sure that my mother was also scared, but she didn't show it. At this point, she had already formulated a strategy that called for our separation to save our lives. She felt that if we went together, we would become too dependent on each other. Then we might not be well oriented or as careful. Besides, she felt that she might become a hindrance because her Polish wasn't as flawless as mine and also that she would slow me down if we had to run. I couldn't agree, but my mother was adamant and quite convinced that individually we would have a better chance for survival. She tried to make me understand that it would be far better if at least one of us were saved than for both of us to perish.

It therefore became necessary to revise our strategy—how I was to leave. I couldn't go wearing that silly gray spring coat, because it was very cold. My mother suggested that I call on the family with whom we had left my fur coat. We hoped that they would return it to me, even though it was just an oral agreement that they hold it for the duration of the war. These people lived in the new section of town that was now under construction. This was where most of the Germans had settled. The buildings were garden apartments, and they were all new. In that area were most of the offices that were erected for the railroad station now taken over by the Germans. It was quite dangerous to enter that area, especially since I had to traverse the entire town to get there. We decided that I would go to see these people the following evening and try to reclaim my fur coat. We talked until late into the night; I was vacillating between weeping and turning a deaf ear to everything. My mother really helped me because she didn't want me to cry too loudly; she cuddled me like a baby. I fell asleep.

The next day, we thought that we were securely hidden in the barn, but our hearts were in our throats whenever the farm children wandered in and out playing all kinds of games. One of these was hide-and-seek and we felt certain they would come up near us because it was an excellent place for them to hide. In two instances a boy came right in front of us but he did not hide in the hay. We held our breaths all through the day and it was difficult to move. When evening came, I was almost paralytically fixed in a permanent position with my knees under my chin. Toward evening when the children were called into the house for supper, I crawled out of the hay, and once again moved towards the railroad tracks and the city.

This time, walking through a different part of the city, I was again intercepted by someone who recognized me. As previously, I had to do a lot of fast talking to convince him to leave me alone and to let me go. It wasn't as difficult this time because this was an older person and I was able to move ahead of him. Finally, I arrived at this family's house (it's strange, but I have forgotten their name) and knocked. They opened the door and looked as if they had seen a ghost. They hesitated for a moment deciding whether or not to let me into the kitchen, but they did. They had two children, a boy and a girl. They gave me food. One of the youngsters stood watch outside the door and the other sat near the table.

When I told them of my plan to leave the city by rail and go to a town where I would not be recognized, they all laughed as they said that there was no chance of getting on the train. Even if I succeeded, they warned me, I would be caught very quickly as I had no papers. I noticed that whenever it came to such situations, everybody had an assortment of negative stories to tell me. They related how a number of people who tried to escape were caught. I said that mother and I had no choice because if we remained there together, the children would find us and deliver us to the Germans. This was the decision reached after long deliberation. After offering me a bowl of soup, the lady returned my fur coat and gave me some dried fruits that I could put in the briefcase that I carried with me. But she refused to let me sleep in their house. Since it was a new garden apartment building, I walked up the stairwell, all the way to the top where a door led out to the roof. There I slept in a little cubicle, waiting until the first light of the morning when I could leave and blend in with the other people going to work.

Later that evening, the third and oldest son of this family (he worked for the railroad) came to visit me. He told me that he heard what I was contemplating. He scared the hell out of me. He regaled me with stories he heard and witnessed on the railroad. He saw the Germans mistreat the Jews, and started to name names. I asked him to please stop, as I really had no choice and that if he really wanted to help me then he should take me along with him next morning when he left for work. No one would think anything about the two of us walking together.

In the early morning he did come for me. I was wearing my fur coat. I felt that as long as no one saw my scared face or noticed my huge overshoes, perhaps no one would suspect anything, especially not the Germans, as by that time the Jews were ordered to divest themselves of fur coats. He left me at the edge of their neighborhood, and very briskly I passed through the side streets of the city. I was very scared because it was getting lighter, and I was afraid that I wouldn't be able to get back to my mother in time. In fact, although it was still fairly dark when we left, by the time I reached the railroad tracks it was much lighter. So for the rest of the day I had to hide out in the haystacks or bushes along the way.

When I finally reached my mother, we cried; this was to be the last day we would spend together. I had some food which I shared with her. It's strange how really unimportant it had become whether we had food or not; a dry piece of bread would last for an entire day. As I remember, the weather was pretty nice at that time so the children played mostly outside and not in the barn. Until then the plan as it was formulated by my mother was that I would leave and try to save myself. However, in my own mind, I really had no idea as to what I wanted to do and where I wanted to go. But during the days when I was hiding out in those various places, I was thinking that a resort area might be safe for me. I reasoned that it was wartime and perhaps many people would not be vacationing.

I decided on Zakopane, a mountain ski resort, where people liked to spend their vacation. I had never been there, but I had heard a lot about it and thought that if I went there, it would be conducive to peace and quiet. There I would try to find a job. At first I thought of tutoring; becoming a maid did not even enter my mind at that point. This being my idea, I talked it over with my mother and she felt that perhaps it did make a lot of sense. However, to travel anywhere in Poland at that time wasn't easy. There were very few places to which one could get a direct train from our small town. The idea was that I would take the train to Lublin and there change to one that would go to Cracow, and from there board a train that would take me to Zakopane. I was very frightened but at least it made me feel better that I had a concrete plan, so that if someone were to ask me, I could tell them where I was going. I didn't have papers, but I didn't even think about that because I felt that no one was going to stop me if I looked confident.

When evening came, the plan had to be implemented. I just couldn't convince myself to leave her, to descend that ladder. She literally had to shove to disengage herself. As I was very slowly going down the ladder, she admonished me to be careful, and advised me to watch what was going on around me, not to act precipitously.

She also said: "You are smart and you will be able to assess a situation very quickly. Don't delay, but act. So if your heart tells you to turn left, don't start thinking that maybe I had better go right. Do what your heart tells you, just go."

Then she said something that I have pondered over for many years, "Do anything anybody asks you to do, just so you save your life."

I couldn't understand what she meant. I said, "Of course I will. I'll work, I'll . . ."

She said, "No, that's not what I meant. If a man wants to hide you and he asks you for anything, you just go ahead and give it to him if it means you can save yourself."

For my mother to say this to me was rather unusual because she was so Victorian, so very straightlaced. When I was dating a young man and she saw us rather close, I was reprimanded. As a teenager I thought that she was old fashioned, very prudish and I was so ultramodern and what did she know. As I think about it now, she was just forty years old, a young woman. The instructions she gave me when we parted were truly a revelation and they became even more meaningful, when months later I was faced with a situation in which I had to make a snap decision about bestowing a sexual favor in exchange for a temporary rescue from the German authorities.

Chapter 7

ATTEMPT TO GET
A POLISH IDENTITY

I CLIMBED DOWN the ladder and opened the door very quietly. I stood outside the barn and couldn't move again. I was panic-stricken, immobilized with fear. A little drizzly snow was falling. I stood there for I can't remember how long. It seemed to me that I was there for an eternity, until I heard something that sounded like the barking of a dog interrupting the quiet of the night. I looked around and decided that I had to start moving.

I have not mentioned the fact that all of the time we were hiding we would hear frequent gunfire and a great number of explosions. Later I learned that these were caused by the Germans. When they were looking for Jews in hiding places, they would not enter the suspected place but would throw a grenade inside to drive out or to kill the people hidden there.

My mother and I decided in the barn while laying out my route that I would not go to the railroad station in Chelm because I might be recognized. We agreed that I would go to the next town, which was Rejowiec. It was a long hike, but I started walking along the wooden crossplanks of the railroad tracks because the earth was soggy and soft from the misty weather. The rhythm of methodical walking seemed to invigorate me. I kept moving at the same pace quickly but in a very measured way which I can still feel now. My body was bent over as I started, but as I marched along at this pace, I began to straighten up, stretching my head upward almost as if I were in a trance.

Finally I arrived at the small train station. It consisted of a tiny room with a little window through which an old man was selling tickets. There were some people standing in the corners, but not enough of them to hide among. I immediately recognized three people who lived in our town; one was a teacher whom I knew, another was the sister of a friend with whom I used to attend public school. None of us acknowledged each other. We all looked away as if we were strangers. I could not understand it but I took a cue from them. I disregarded them and at the window I asked for a ticket to Cracow. I was told that I would have to buy a ticket to Lublin, change trains there, and buy the ticket to Cracow.

I asked, "Are you sure? Is there nothing I can do to avoid changing trains?"

It was night now, and the ticket agent replied, "If the train arrives at a certain time, they may shuttle it over. So I will give you a ticket to Cracow but you will have to listen for their announcement. Either that train will continue, or they will connect it to another. It is up to you to watch where you are going."

The train arrived about a half hour later. I boarded it; I found that it was quite crowded and it was difficult to find a seat. I noticed that the two other Jewish people I had recognized at the station went in another direction. They boarded a different car than the one I did. I supposed each of us thought that we looked more non-Jewish than the others. If they were gentiles, they would probably have said something to me. But they were Jewish and most likely had a similar thought, that of moving to a larger city where they would not, in all likelihood, be recognized. I finally found a seat where I was squeezed between a peasant lady and a man who looked as if he were an official. It was dark and it was difficult to move about, since the lights were switched off.

Before we entered Lublin, the train was held up at a stop signal. The rumor was that the train was stopped because the SS men were conducting an examination to ascertain the cause of a derailment. The Poles who sat on both sides of me and across from me were saying, "Oh, of course, there must be many Jews on this train and they are coming to hunt them down."

The train moved for a while, then stopped again. When it finally entered the Lublin station, we heard many German voices, those of Gestapo soldiers. They yelled that nobody, not even those disembarking at Lublin, was allowed to leave the train until the Germans arrived and checked everyone's papers. Then I realized that I was in trouble. I knew I had nothing to show, and there was no reasoning with the Germans. I was sitting farthest from the door. A woman was seated near the window, I was next to her and further on there was a man. The Germans scurried about; they started from the side opposite me and everyone showed their papers. Then they made a U-turn and came back up the aisle towards me. When they reached the man, who I assumed was an official, and who apparently was also traveling without the proper documents, they became so busy dragging him off the train that they left our compartment. They wanted a *Kenncarte* or I.D. card, which was a document that certified that one was not Jewish, and that the bearer had been an Aryan for at least five past generations. This man did possess some papers and did produce them, but somehow the Germans were not completely satisfied with them and became so involved that I and the lady at the end were not questioned. I don't know why I didn't faint. The more the man argued, the more unconvincing he became until the Germans removed him bodily from the train, and, once they left, they never returned. My car was eventually connected to the main train and sped on to Cracow.

I didn't think I'd be able to keep my composure, but the peasant woman sitting next to me was very chatty and she kept talking incessantly. Everybody was quite involved in what had happened. Their opinions were divided: "It served him right." . . . "He's a Jew." . . . "He shouldn't lie." Others defended him. These discussions went on for a couple of hours until everyone got tired and fell asleep. The rest of the trip to Cracow was quite uneventful.

When I arrived in Cracow, I was exhausted. I didn't know where to go nor what to do. I had to get to Zakopane but I was famished. It was late in the afternoon when I walked out of the railroad station, and it was already quite dark. In my elegant fur coat, I meandered through the streets. I carried the blanket that I was given; it was actually a bedcover, maroon on one side and cream colored on the other, certainly incongruous for one in a fur coat. As I passed the houses, I looked in the windows, thinking about the lights behind the curtains and the people who lived there. I felt sorry for myself and I was very hungry. Then I decided, "What the hell, I have a couple of hundred zloty, I will go into a restaurant and have something to eat!" I walked into the first one I saw. There were very few non-Germans present and there were many soldiers. I backed out because I was afraid to sit in the restaurant with them. Someone might engage me in conversation and ask questions. There was a little grocery nearby where I bought bread and a piece of salami. I went back to the railroad station and got a drink at a stand.

I found a bench and sat down. After I finished eating, I really didn't know what to do with myself. Then I thought that since this was such a huge station, I would utilize the facilities to take a shower. In the bathroom I looked at my clothes. They were awful. My sweater was dirty but I had no choice—I didn't have a change, and I couldn't wash anything. I did have clean underwear and I wrapped the underwear I had been wearing, hoping that somehow, somewhere, I would be able to launder them. I returned to the main hall of the station where everybody waited, and by this time all the benches were occupied. I looked for a place on the floor and found one. I spread my blanket and sat down in one of the corners.

It didn't take long before a lady, Mrs. Bogdanowa, became very chummy and asked me where I was going. I concocted a story about my being the daughter of a Polish couple of the intelligentsia and that I belonged to an organization that opposed the German occupation. Now that the authorities had "cleaned out" the Jewish population, they started after the intelligentsia to prevent them from organizing a resistance movement. I told her that my father was a professor and that he had been arrested. I told her that my mother had sent me away because she was afraid that I would be the next target as my family had tried to organize some opposition. The lady sat and shook her head repeatedly and asked me where I was going. I told her that I had thought of moving on to Zakopane for a couple of weeks and then I would see how long my money would last.

She looked at me and said, "Don't you know about Zakopane?"

I asked, "What should I know about Zakopane?"

She replied, "The Germans have converted this resort into a rest camp where soldiers are sent to recuperate. You are entering a hornet's nest if you go there. Besides, you won't find any place to stay, nor would you find any employment there."

I said, "I am still going. I am too tired to make any other arrangements."

She was quiet for a moment and then said, "You know what, I am going on business." This meant that she would travel to small villages to barter clothing and merchandise that she acquired from Jewish people in the ghetto in exchange for butter and eggs. She then supplemented her profits through the sale of chickens and other foodstuffs to the grocers. She gave me her address, and suggested that when my vacation was over I should look her up in the event I decided to return to Cracow.

I said, "Fine."

We were compelled to stay in the station until morning, as a curfew was in force and nobody, not Jews nor anyone else was permitted in the streets. At five o'clock when the train arrived, I purchased a ticket and boarded the train to Zakopane.

The station in that town was very small. I walked out into the street, passed some small houses and continued on toward the center of town. In the station I had noticed a sign advertising a room for rent and when I reached the address, I saw a small house with a little veranda enclosed in glass. A short, thin man answered my knock and asked what I wanted. I told him that I had seen the sign in the station and that I was here to inquire about the vacancy. He led me into the living room, and sat down at a table looking at me.

He said, "Why don't you go to a hotel?"

I said, "Look, I heard that there are many German soldiers here and I have already had my share of sad experiences, among them my father's arrest. I therefore don't wish to go to a hotel where soldiers congregate. All I want is a little peace and quiet for two weeks or so."

He answered, "Oh, two weeks, I don't know . . ."

Quickly I added, "It depends, actually. I'll probably stay longer, if my mother sends me more money. In the meantime, I have enough funds for perhaps a month."

This dispelled his indecision. "All right, a month is okay." Then he placed a book before me, saying: "We don't have a regular registration procedure as in a hotel, but I have to account for my rental for tax purposes so I keep a list of the people who stay here in this book. What is your name?"

My mind went blank. I unexplainably could not think of any name. I could have used my own; it probably would have been all right. Even though I was raised in a neighborhood of Polish people and had two close girlfriends who lived next door, I couldn't think of one single Polish name to give him.

He looked at me and shook his head, "Look lady, I don't think you should stay here. I don't believe that I should take any chances with you. I think you are Jewish."

I said, "Oh no, I'm not. It's just that I have had such a shock, such a difficult time with the authorities."

But he said, "I am sorry. I can't rent the room to you."

I was devastated, but he continued, "Get out of here and fast! I don't want anything to do with you."

So I walked out and moved on down the street, hoping to see another "For Rent" sign. As I went on, there, coming towards me was a young man whom I recognized from my hometown. He had been in the class ahead of me in gimnazium.

He was not Jewish. I became terribly frightened and walked hurriedly to the other side of the street so I could avoid his seeing me. I returned to the railroad station and immediately decided that I would go back to Cracow to visit that lady I had met and try to arrange something with her.

When I arrived at the small Zakopane train station, I looked over the train schedule and learned that another train was not due for a couple of hours. So I had a little something to eat and waited. I was very upset at the possibility of meeting someone who might know me. But it never happened. Eventually I boarded the train back to Cracow. It was late in the afternoon and I didn't think that at that time I could manage to call on the lady. I wasn't quite certain of her address or how to get there. By that time I was hungry again and ventured out onto the streets in the vicinity of the main Cracow station. I decided that I would return to the station before it was closed for curfew. Now that the railroad station had become a kind of a haven for me, I knew that there were a number of hours that I could spend there undisturbed, and during that time I could plan my strategy and my next moves.

I returned to the station, trying to figure out what to do next. When I got there, there wasn't a vacant bench available. People were walking about looking for the most desirable places to sit other than the benches. These were in the corners of the various rooms, but they too were taken. After much searching I found a little nook. I sat down and tried to think of a reason I could give the lady for not being able to stay in Zakopane. What excuse could I offer that would sound acceptable to her? The station gates were locked and it became very quiet in the station. People tried to sleep sitting or standing; some were able to lie down. I was very uncomfortable because the way I was dressed belied my circumstances. Here I was, wearing an elegant fur coat and fine hat sitting on the floor on a blanket with my knees under my chin. However I couldn't worry about that. After a while my mind became a blank; I really didn't know what to do. Eventually I fell asleep and woke when I started to hear movement near me. People were rising and moving toward the main gate. I realized that the curfew would be over shortly and everyone pressed toward the door because there were many peasants who came to Cracow to sell their wares.

I also started to march around the station still unsure of what to do. As I was pacing, I noticed that a woman had vacated a place on a bench, I sat down immediately. I was tired and uncomfortable, but the position in which I now sat was a little more relaxing and I closed my eyes. Then I heard the locks on the doors being opened and it seemed as if a vacuum cleaner was sucking the people out of the station, so quickly were people leaving the building. I was panic-stricken, realizing that I would have to go and I still hadn't decided what to do. I started to cry. I hadn't done so since I left my mother a couple of days earlier. I stored up so much emotion that I tried to control. Now my entire body was aquiver from sobbing. The woman next to me put her arms about me and tried to find out why I was behaving in this way. Through the tears I couldn't really express myself and somehow I heard her say, "Did somebody steal something from you? Did anything happen to you?"

And as she tried to console me, I thought that I should say that my pocketbook containing my papers was stolen and I didn't know what to do. Then curiously this woman, who was trying to be helpful, said, "Oh, I assume that the lady who was sitting on the other side of you must have been a Jew and must have noticed that you had the papers and took them from you."

Within five minutes, three other people swore that they saw a woman take my pocketbook. They even described it. I actually had my envelope-type pocketbook in my briefcase. But this woman said that it was a pocketbook with two handles, and however else anyone described it, I said, "Yes. Yes. . . . and it was black and was made of beautiful leather."

As a crowd gathered around me, an SS patrolman came by and asked, "What happened?" I repeated the story as the people had told it to me. He expressed some pity and said he was very sorry for me. I asked, "What do I do now?"

He said that he didn't know whether he could do anything for me, but that around the corner, about a block down, was the Polish police precinct station. He suggested that I go there and report my losses so that they could start a procedure by which I would either retrieve the papers or get duplicates. Of course, I said that I had a great deal of money in my purse and somebody else said that perhaps it was not the papers but the money that they wanted and that they would probably throw the papers away.

With a heavy heart I went to the police station. The Polish officer on duty was not as sympathetic as the German officer had been. He looked at me as if to say, "Ha, you are making up the story." He said: "Are you sure this is what happened? Or is this just a story you concocted?"

By this time, I was still crying but less intensely. I began believing in the plausibility of the story. I insisted on the veracity of my story, and he asked me to wait. Then someone entered with a secretary who took down my entire deposition.

Another officer said: "Well, it doesn't sound right to me. It appears that you are making this up." Then he added: "Bear in mind that before anything can be done they will check with Chelm if such a person really exists."

This time, on the way from the railroad station to the police, I had already selected a name; it was Maria, the girl in whose house I tried to hide on the night of the Judenrein assault. I knew a great deal about her, so I thought. I used to do some of the paperwork for her mother, consisting of reports to city hall. The young lady would visit her aunt out of town, and Poland required that each time we moved to another town a change of address report was obligatory. I was familiar with her birthdate, her place of birth, her name, and other germane information. Now as the officer noted all the personal data, I appropriated the name of Maria Dzwigaj. I submitted the name of Mr. Dzwigaj as her father because that was the one they used on the papers that I would fill out for them in Chelm.

The officer took it all down as I sat there waiting, thinking he was going to give me a piece of paper to present to the lady whom I planned to visit. This, I was convinced, would not receive the same rejection as in Zakopane. But the man said, "Look, we are not issuing any papers to you at this time. It will take at least three days for us to check out the information. We'll have to call Chelm to ascertain whether Mr. and Mrs. Dzwigaj exist, if the address is correct and whether Maria is their daughter."

I had no choice. I turned and walked out. Outside I asked a policeman how I could get to the address of Mrs. Bogdanowa, the woman I wanted to see. He told me I had to take two buses. It was almost on the periphery of the city. The area seemed newly developed; there were new projects, new houses not very tall, about three or four stories. I wandered through the neighborhood before I found her house. It seemed like a lower middle class area. I didn't notice many people, as it was early morning. There were no children about; they were probably all in school. I entered the building, and looked for her apartment number because she had not given it to me. I could not find it on the tenants' listing and kept looking.

Suddenly I heard a tapping on the basement window. I looked down and saw the lady. She had coincidentally been looking out of the window and seen me. She invited me into the house. Her husband was the janitor in the building and they lived in one large room. The bed was in one corner and the kitchen in the other. A large table in the center divided the room and I saw another bed on one side. At once my heart started to pound as I saw no possibility of having a place in this one-room dwelling. But she was very prescient and she noticed my roving eye. She said, "No, don't worry, we have a portable screen and there is a bed we can open. Don't worry, we will put you up here."

She was very eager to learn what had happened as she could gather from my swollen eyes that I had been crying. I told her that someone had stolen my purse and taken my papers. She shook her head but seemed skeptical. The next thing she asked was whether all of my money was gone. I said that I had another smaller purse that I carried separately in case of such an eventuality. I told her that I still had enough money to last for the couple of weeks that I would have to stay in Cracow. She accepted this explanation and asked whether I was hungry and when I last ate, as it was two days and one night since I had last seen her. I said yes, I had eaten something, but she asked, "Well, if you want me to cook something, I do not have any money right now and if you would let me have some, I will buy food for supper."

And so, like the VIP that I wasn't, I went to my purse, took out a brand new hundred zloty bill and told her that whatever I had in smaller currency wouldn't be enough and I would need the change anyway so she should buy whatever she needed. At that time almost everything had to be bought on the black market. I suggested that before she left she should boil some water so that I could wash and by the time she returned I would be done. She was, as I have said, a very clever lady, and a godsend to me, like a guardian angel. She left, and although the grocery was not that far away, she did not return for about an hour. That gave me time to take care of my hygiene.

I did not wash in her room. She had taken me to a section of the basement near the boiler, pointed to a little space, taken out a huge basin, and told me to use it to wash myself. This was my first opportunity to wash, other than the makeshift shower I took when I first came to Cracow. I had been wearing the same clothes for a long time. And when I removed them, they were full of lice. I had never been in such a situation before and I panicked. But I said to myself, "If you react in this way, you will open yourself to suspicion and that could be dangerous." I sat there and prayed that she would not come back before I was finished. I cleaned my sweater as best I could. The seams were lice infested. I was young and had never been exposed to this parasite, but somehow one knows instinctively just what to do. My turtle-necked sweater was maroon, one that I had embroidered with blue thread. The entire embroidery on the inside of the sweater was a nesting place for bugs. I cleaned it as adequately as I could, went back to the kitchen and put up a smaller pot of water. As I did this, I thought that if I used that hot liquid on the sweater it would shrink, but if I didn't I would suffer the agony of being at the mercy of the lice. But perhaps I could stretch it. I had already rinsed my underwear and other things in the boiled water. I waited until it cooled a little. She had still not returned. I then washed the sweater, soaking and stretching it on a towel that was already wet. I put on a bathrobe that I carried in my attaché case; it was made of striped flannel, short, with red, blue, and white stripes, and it was a rather new acquisition. I remember my mother saying, when we were leaving: "Take along everything that is new because you don't know how long you may have to wear it."

By the time Mrs. Bogdanowa came home, I was scrubbed and cleaned, and my hair and clothing washed. She was quite pleased. I didn't know how to be more convincing about my papers, and I wasn't sure that she had believed my story. I wasn't comfortable as a liar. As I was sitting with her, waiting for the oatmeal she was preparing, which would "stick to my ribs," I amended the entire tale, stressing the fact that there were other people who had witnessed the incident, and five of these had testified to the German examiner. Then I said: "I have to return to the police station in three days." I saw that she was worried. I asked her to allow me to stay with her for at least the three days that I would have to wait to receive my new documents.

She said, "Don't worry."

I asked, "Do you want me to pay in advance for the extra time? How much do you want?"

We settled this and I paid her. I was really much too generous at that point. Later when my funds started running low, I felt that perhaps I should have spent only about half the amount. She appreciated my generosity; she knew that after the three days, if I was caught, she already had the money, so all that she would have to do would be to put up with me for those three days. When I was through with eating, she prepared my bed. I fell asleep, and did not wake for twenty-four hours.

When I rose, it was evening and there were people sitting around the table. They were neighbors playing cards. I heard them talking and I assumed it was about me. Here I was lying in that corner. She had given me a cover; my fur coat was over that because it was quite cold in the basement. They said that she was stupid, that she would get caught for harboring a Jew. She replied that she had asked all kinds of questions and I had convinced her of my veracity. She said, "I am not easily fooled, and I would know a Jew if I saw one." The husband, who was an elderly gentleman and was, from what I learned, a drunkard, was non-committal as long as the money was available. He reasoned that even if I were caught, they would have nothing to worry about.

I feigned sleep until everybody left the room. Then I rose and she served me tea and something to eat. I had only a day and a half left of my extension. During that time we would talk, although most of the time I slept rather fitfully. Two days had passed uneventfully.

Chapter 8

LIFE WITH THE
LOHO FAMILY IN CRACOW

THE MORNING ARRIVED when I finally had to report to the police. My landlady woke me with a cheery "Good morning. Today is yours, Maria. You've got to pick up your papers. I hope everything works out well for you."

She gave me good travel directions and I left for the police station. I was extremely nervous and very scared. I hoped that the officers would be far too busy to bother with an in-depth check. Besides, a telephone call to another government office for verification would really not be a probability. Should they write and ask for the return of papers, it would take more than three days, so I doubted that they would use that method. I further reasoned that they most likely would try to confirm, but they might simply call my bluff. If I were really Jewish and had made up the story, they would feel sure that I would not risk coming back for the papers. When I did return, the same officer was on duty. It was early in the morning. The officer smiled sarcastically, "Oh, you're back."

I said, "Yes, why shouldn't I be here? My papers were stolen."

He replied, "Oh, so they were really stolen?"

"Yes, they were." He sent me to another office and once again they took down my story. This time I was a little calmer and more coherent. They then filled out a form verifying that Maria Dzwigaj, born on such-and-such a date, and in such-and-such a town, came to Cracow on this specific date, claiming that her papers were stolen and that this was a substitute document to help her initiate the process of receiving a new *Kennkarte*. A large notary public stamp and seal of the German Reich made this an official certificate. My hands shook as it was handed to me. I read it but did not notice all the minute details. I knew that all the basic information and signatures were included, and that was enough for me. With that paper in hand, I went to a grocery next door and bought some food to serve for the celebration I planned. I took the bus back.

Mrs. Bogdanowa was thoroughly convinced, took the paper and ran to her next door neighbor to prove that I really was not lying. I remained there for one more day and then she said: "Look, my dear friend, I have to go out into the country on business. I have lots of merchandise to sell. I am scheduled to go on a trip, and I am sorry, but with my husband who is a drunkard and without a room with a door to lock yourself in, I don't think it is safe for you to stay here. Perhaps when he is sober, he might not harm you, but when he's drunk, I can't take the responsibility for him. So you had better find yourself another place."

Again, I was faced with making a decision about what to do. In three days, I had already been lulled into complacency. I thought that I was safe, and at least for the time being, I would be able to relax. But when she said this the tension returned and I stiffened. I lost track of time until she said: "Don't worry. I suggest that you go to the railroad station. There are all sorts of bulletin boards throughout the place. Look them over. People advertise rooms for rent. Many of the peasants who come to the city do not wish to check into hotels because they come to conduct illegal business and do not want to be traced. Go there and I am sure you will find what you are looking for. You can also ask a redcap, because some of them know of available places in the neighborhood near the railroad station."

I left my briefcase and blanket behind and took the bus into the city. Again, I walked around the railroad station, my haven conducive to thinking. I didn't find anything that appealed to me on the boards. I approached a redcap, a gray-haired avuncular-looking elderly man, and told him that I needed to stay in Cracow for a couple of days and did he know of anything available. If he would help me find some quarters, I would reward him with a sum of money for his efforts. I told him that the renter he recommended would also probably give him something. He agreed, and told me that I should stay around until he finished his work at three o'clock when he would be able to accompany me to a couple of homes he knew about, where there were rooms for rent. He later led me to three or four places, but one was already taken, and another looked at me and said he didn't want me. He finally couldn't go with me any longer, but he gave me another address and said that they didn't rent rooms there, only beds for the night, which would probably cost less than paying for a room.

This apartment was located in the backyard of a building. It resembled what I would describe as a motel. It was built around a central square with terraces all about. I walked up a flight of stairs, and rang the bell. An elderly lady opened the door. She looked me over and asked a few questions. I told her what by now had become my routine story, that I am away from my town on business in Cracow and I would like to remain here a few nights, or as long as it would take for me to consummate my business transaction. She told me that she only rents beds; she had a room and a hall and a little alcove furnished with several beds. The main room with a window is only rented to men. It so happened there were two beds occupied by two men, but she did have an alcove with one bed available, which she could let me have. Her price was twenty zloty per night. That was a great deal of money at that time, but I was happy to get it. She asked for my name and told me that curfew was at seven o'clock and she expected me to be there at six or before. If I was not on time she would rent to someone else to avoid losing twenty zloty for the bed. I said "Of course I'll be on time."

I still had about two and one-half hours to spare, so I surely hoped to be on time as it would take me about thirty minutes to return to the former landlady's home. I went back there and started packing my briefcase. Mrs. Bogdanowa said, "You know what—I am leaving by train. Why don't you wait five minutes and we will go together since I too am traveling in the same direction."

I agreed to wait for her. I always felt safer with somebody who was Polish and self-assured. We waited a long time for the bus, which then moved along very slowly. By the time I came back to my lodging it was past the deadline. When I opened the door, it was already dark; the woman stood there and said "Oh, I'm sorry. . . . we already rented your bed."

It is true, she had stressed the importance of being back in time. I stood there perplexed, not knowing what to do. While the woman was talking to me, her daughter, perhaps in her late twenties, and her little boy, came into the kitchen. They looked at me. I said that I had already checked out from where I had stayed previously and couldn't return. And I told them that I had stayed with an acquaintance whose husband is a drunkard, and she had warned me that it was not a safe place for me. By the time we finished talking, it was about fifteen minutes before curfew and I noticed that the little boy was tugging at his mother's skirt. She was not paying attention to him as she was listening intently to my story and I must have made it quite evident that I was really upset. Finally, they told the boy to stop annoying them, but he insisted, "I have something to say." So the grandmother told him to speak and then get out of there, "Grandma, this is such a small lady and I have such a big crib and where are you going to send her out into the dark." It was cold, raining, and snowing. "Why can't she sleep in my crib and I will stay with Mommy, then tomorrow maybe somebody will leave and she can have the bed."

The two women looked at each other and smiled. It was such a nice, warm, and really sympathetic reaction. They may have been money-hungry but they appeared to be sympathetic, not angry. They decided to implement the boy's suggestion, and he was really quite excited over the fact that they listened to him. They were very supportive and praised him for performing his good deed. I was told where

I could hang my outer garments. The little boy followed me closely and asked all kinds of questions . . . did I know this story, that one, did I know how to sing? I was then invited to sit down at the table with the whole family group—grandmother, grandfather, their daughter, and her son and her daughter, who was a little older than the boy. Her name was Jadwiga, his Andrzej. They were both very beautiful children. I was told that the little boy had a fine ear for music; he could play any melody on the piano at age five. He was a young genius and they all loved him for his talent. Later on, he and I spent a great deal of time at the piano; he played and I sang.

After the children left to get ready for bed, the grandfather, Mr. Loho, said, "This is not a hotel and we are not required to submit reports, but we do keep books for our own protection, and I would like you to register. Please let me see your papers."

I showed him the document that I had. As I related my story, he sat there in his slippers, shaking his head. He looked at the paper and then at me. Once again the children came to my rescue, "Hey, Grandpa, what are you thinking? She is nice, let her stay, please let her stay."

So he said, "Well, I don't care, I'm sure you're not going to stay with us for that long a time but I don't know if this document is legitimate."

I said "Do believe me, it is absolutely authentic." I then told my story again. In all of the excitement, I had forgotten to eat, I was that upset. They gave me a cup of tea and a little biscuit. I went to sleep in the large crib that was almost like a small bed. In that one huge room there were two huge double beds; Mr. and Mrs. Loho slept in one corner and the mother and daughter in the other bed. The crib was near the door.

In the early dawn I heard somebody knocking on the railing of the bed: "Maria, it is early in the morning and in order to get the milk and other dairy products for the children, we must rise at break of day. The grocer knows us and will fill our order before he officially opens the store, otherwise I will have to wait in line. Could we have your rent money for our shopping?"

I handed her twenty zloty. She looked at me and said: "Well, this is not really a bed so we will charge you only ten zloty for the use of the crib. Tonight we will supply a bed and for that you will pay twenty."

I turned around and tried to fall asleep but before I knew it, the little boy was in the crib asking me to sing a song. For almost an entire hour we sat together. He kept requesting me to tell him stories and to sing songs. He had immediately taken a fancy to me. He finally allowed me to get dressed and when I came out of the main bedroom, all the beds were made, and the house began to resemble a home, not a shelter. The windows were open. I dressed and said I was going out to get something to eat. The little boy was sitting at the table but he refused to eat; he asked me to sing him a song.

During the months that followed, he developed an attachment to me and would not touch his food unless I ate with him; he refused to go to bed unless I tucked him in and he clung to me for dear life all of the time. The reason may have been that his grandmother was busy with the housework and the cooking, his grandfather and his mother were radiologists; both worked long hours. This child then had no one with whom to play and since I enjoyed playing, was young and remembered poetry and lots of folk songs, I was glad to indulge him. In appreciation, I was often offered a cup of tea, and when I said I was going out for something to eat, they also offered me breakfast.

Everyday I dressed and left for the city. I went into town for no particular reason. I pretended that I had to attend to some business. When I saw lines in front of soup kitchens, I joined the queue in my fancy fur coat and had soup. Later, I found another place and had a second bowl. That's how I sustained myself. I estimated how much money I had and how long it was going to last including the expense for my bed. This went on for perhaps a week or so. When I returned I would be asked what I had accomplished, and I always concocted some story. While I was in the city, I would always pay attention to lines that were forming, usually for food. I figured that if they gave something away at either a discount or gratis, I would get it. That's how I was able to get cheese or whatever they dispensed that day. Roaming through the streets, I also visited the churches. I would enter them because the Germans seldom assaulted anyone there. I would sit in a pew, pretending I was praying or contemplating. When it was cold outdoors, the inside of a church was a warm place to be. I went to several churches so as not to draw suspicion to myself. This went on for weeks.

Each evening all sorts of people would gather at the house in which I stayed. There were some peasants, some members of the intelligentsia. A man who slept in the main room appeared to be a Jewish professional who was also masquerading as I was, but no one asked any questions; they were only interested in the money. Little Andrzej was very musical. His father was a pianist, his uncle was a musician; there was a lot of music in the family. The children's father was a POW in Auschwitz; he had been an officer in the Polish Army who had in some way displeased the Germans. So the family was somewhat empathetic now though they were non-Jewish. The grandmother told me that she was a distant relative of a famous Polish painter Jan Matejko. They prided themselves on being professionals and belonging to a better class.

Sometimes, when the weather was very bad, and in November it was, I did not stray too far from the house. My decision to go into the city was usually made spontaneously. I spent a great deal of time in the house, and decided that while I was there, I wouldn't be idle, so I worked with the grandmother in the kitchen. I helped her clean, make the beds, and at one point she said: "You know you are going to sleep in a bed, but I am going to charge you less because you have been so helpful."

One day she complained about a backache, and was unable to scrub the kitchen floor. I said: "I know that you are not feeling well and I do not have much to do. I can go to the city an hour later. Would you permit me to scrub the floor for you?"

She refused at first, but then agreed. She left the kitchen, and I went down on my knees and started to scrub. Mrs. Loho walked in to see what I was doing and her first words were, "Oh my God, what kind of a Jewish job are you doing?"

My heart started pounding so heavily I thought it would jump out of my mouth. Luckily I was on my hands and knees and was able to bend down so that she wouldn't notice that I had become pale and I said, "What do you mean?"

She said, "That's not how you wash a floor!"

I exclaimed, "You'll have to excuse me. I never did this before."

She taught me the proper method. I'm a pretty good learner and eventually became an expert. After washing the floors and straightening out the beds, I began to rise at five a.m. to buy the groceries, and to stand on line so that I saved Mrs. Loho some work. One evening we were sitting at home and she said jokingly, "You know what, a neighbor next door engaged me in a friendly argument because I purchased some eggs from a peasant from whom she wanted to buy."

It seems that the two neighbors weren't too fond of each other. "Hmmm, now you are a pretty smart lady. Not only do you rent rooms but you manage to influence people to perform chores for you. You engage a maid and pay nothing. What kind of a person are you?"

The neighbor had cast an aspersion on Mrs. Loho's character. They had discussed it in a jocular manner. But with me it was rather serious, I really didn't like the fact that someone else was aware of my presence, and that it was undoubtedly known to others. In the meantime, since it was the end of November, they began planning for Christmas. I was quite knowledgeable about all the preliminary activities attendant upon Christmas. We discussed the traditional menus and planned the meal. In the meantime, the Loho family started to prod me: "Did you get your birth certificate from the church? Because unless you have one, you cannot apply for your papers." I assured them that I had indeed requested a copy of my certificate.

During the day I took the children for a walk out of doors. On Sunday I attended church with them and I also went along to Mass when the grandmother was too tired and the mother needed a rest after working the entire week. One day I returned and I noticed that there was a lot of tension in the house. I really couldn't understand it and no one was saying anything because I was with the children, and it was time for the boy to eat. I sensed that something was wrong. When the child went to bed, I sat down at the table in the outside room where we would all congregate. Mr. Loho, the grandfather, approached me and tossed a postcard on a table. It was postmarked from the parish where I had applied for my birth certificate. In answer to my request the priest wrote that no person named Maria Dzwigaj was ever born there. Now that upset me, because I knew that it was her birthplace, since I had done a great deal of paperwork for that family. I said, "I don't know what's wrong. There must be some mistake. I will check it out."

Early next morning, I went to the post office and placed a person-to-person call to the mother of Maria in Chelm, to ask her what was happening. This was an involved procedure. But I knew that the Dzwigaj family did not live far from the post office and I was told that I would have an answer within two hours. So I had to wait there for two hours and when the call finally came through, it was the father who was called to the phone. The mother was out taking care of business. The father was perturbed and angry. First of all, he berated me for endangering his life by calling him. So I said, "You know who I am, but I used a different name, the post office does not know me, and they cannot possibly know my true identity. Calm down, I want to know what the story is on Maria. I tried to get a copy of her birth certificate and was told that nobody was ever baptized by that name in this church."

In spite of his anger, he started to laugh and said, "Because you are stupid. Maria is not my daughter. She is her mother's out-of-wedlock child; she was baptized under the name Klimczak rather than Dzwigaj because I didn't even know her mother at the time. We were never married. We live like a couple but we were never wed."

Well, this was a relief. Then he said: "You know, Mrs. Dzwigaj has a sister who lives outside of Cracow. Your mother came to us and left some clothing for you. My wife gave it to her sister and so maybe her sister will bring it to you."

I said, "All right." He added, "Don't you ever call me again because it is too risky to talk with you."

I went home quite upset, facing a new dilemma. The name I was using was not the correct one. What was I going to do? I came home looking very worried, which was quite apparent to everyone because I always appeared so happy-go-lucky, a trait which was an integral part of my personality. I sat down with the family, the grandmother, the grandfather, and the mother. I told them that I was never told that I was not my father's daughter, I naturally assumed that I was. These people's questions were: "What do you mean? You never heard any mention in the house? Didn't you soon learn that he moved in later?" They cross-examined me. I told them that it really wasn't something I wanted to know. And I certainly wouldn't have taken such a great risk when I needed to receive my new papers, to use a wrong name. I asked them what they thought I should do now. Since they were quite skeptical, they advised me to write to the priest again and to repeat what I told them. I did so.

For a week or so, I enjoyed a little peace because everyone was waiting for the reply to my letter. They were fairly certain that I was not telling the truth. But eventually, the birth certificate did come in the name of Maria Klimczak. The tension eased in the home. I was now a person who existed, who was certifiably born. In the meantime, the neighbor who used to quarrel with Mrs. Loho, the grandmother, started to pressure these people and threatened to go to the police to report that the Lohos were operating a rooming house and harboring undesirable elements. This, even though she was doing the same thing: renting beds. She felt that the Lohos found a "gold mine," that they received more money than she did. She was particularly envious of my caring for the children. I was younger, well-dressed, and the youngsters probably bragged about me to their playmates. Others among them were also envious because Andrzej and Jadwiga had a governess who taught, played with, and sang for them. So the neighbors began threatening to report them to the police. During the several conferences I had with the Lohos, they said that perhaps I had better find a job and cease to jeopardize them any longer. At that point, the fact that I had changed my name was already illegal and I might get into further difficulties. I don't know whether they suspected that I was Jewish. However, they adored that little boy. Whatever he wanted, he received. When he asked me to eat supper, I did so. My money was not being depleted and I was not charged for each meal I ate in the house.

In addition, I sometimes helped my hosts earn extra money by letting them rent out my bed, while I slept in little Andrzej's crib.

Chapter 9

MAID TO AN SS MAN

I STARTED LOOKING in the papers to see what jobs were available. I found an ad for a job in a new section of Cracow. I called for an appointment and was told to come over for an interview.

I went there in the afternoon. The name was a Polish-sounding one, Sierecki, and the woman was about my age, petite and vivacious. She invited me into the living room. She remarked that I did not look like a maid. I said, "Does a maid look any special way?"

"Oh, stop kidding. You know what I mean. I have had many; I just lost one. She stole many items from the house, and she was a peasant who hardly spoke any German. You talk like a cultured German, you are dressed like a person who comes from the city and not a village. You seem quite sophisticated."

"Yes, sure I am educated. My family, however, is experiencing some difficulties and I can't remain with them. I have to stay in Cracow."

She said; "Why don't you get a job in an office?"

I said, "Such a position doesn't pay very much. I don't possess that many office skills. Beside, I need money not only for food, but for rent."

"You are wearing an expensive fur coat. Why don't you sell it for your monetary needs?" she retorted.

I said, "It is rather difficult to rent an apartment. And even if I sold the coat, I would need another one."

"Well, would you sell it to me? Let me try it on." It fit quite well.

"I will sell it to you if you give me in exchange a nice cloth coat, and the job. I would like it to be a sleep-in position."

She smiled, "You are quite clever." I thanked her for the compliment.

"This may present a problem because I am going to visit my parents in Köln and we don't have an extra room for a maid. We do have an alcove in the kitchen where we can set up a bed and draw a curtain around it. Furthermore, I don't think it would be proper for you to remain home alone with Werner, my husband. There is no point in continuing our discussion, since my husband would have to approve the agreement. Could you please come back in the morning at about eight o'clock, before he leaves for work?"

He was an editor of a section of the major Polish newspaper in Cracow. I said I would come tomorrow morning.

I returned to the house and informed the Loho family that I had a good possibility of securing a job and it was in a nice three-room apartment, with a small bedroom, a living room, and a kitchen; a very nice modern home. It looked neat and tidy and the young couple would be just right for me. They all expressed their hope that I would secure the position.

The next day I arrived at eight o'clock in the morning. The door was opened by a large, handsome man in an SS uniform with an SS insignia on the black velvet collar. It was Mr. Sierecki. The woman with whom I had spoken yesterday was petite and dark-haired. He was tall, blond, and blue-eyed. Hanging in the foyer was his long green SS uniform coat and a very well-made SS hat. The sight of the Gestapo uniform frightened me. I was hardly able to speak.

He was having coffee; his wife was still sleeping. Before he even looked at my papers he said, "I hope you realize that if you are Jewish and if we find out, your life will be worthless." He told me what he could do, and called me to the window on their third floor, showed me the backyard and the stand on which the carpets are beaten clean. "See the black spots down there. They are blood. A colonel who lives across the hall from us employed a Jewish girl as a maid. And when he discovered that fact, he didn't arrest her, but took her right down to the courtyard and shot her. If you're Jewish and we find out, you too will be killed."

He asked me for an I.D. I related the story of my papers and showed him what I had. He said, "But this is only a statement, not the document. You had eight weeks to get new papers and the time has already passed." I repeated the story about the name change, and that I was not aware that I was born out-of-wedlock. He shook his head, his icy blue eyes looking right through me seemingly saying, "Well, I hope you know what you are talking about because if we check it out, and find that you lied, you will die."

I said, "Look, I have told you the truth. That's the way it is. That's what I am doing in Cracow. I need the job. My family . . ."

I had a hard time keeping track of what I was telling him. I knew that I had to be consistent, I didn't really deviate from my original story, but I embellished it a little as I repeated it. He looked at me: "Hmmm, my wife Charlotte was impressed with your coat."

"What do you mean?"

"She wants it!"

Then I thought maybe she had softened him up. "Well, I will gladly give it to her because it is just not the proper attire for a maid."

"All right, wait until she rises. I have no objections, and if she craves your coat and wants it, the job is yours. Besides, if they catch you as a Jew, she will get the coat anyhow. Since she recommends you highly, you may work here. She did mention to you that she is going to Köln next week and you definitely will not be able to stay while she is away."

He was not too supportive, but he wasn't entirely negative. He was probably brainwashed by the wife. I felt that at least now I had a foot in the door. He finished eating and left for work. The wife came out of the bedroom and led me into a built-in closet; it was the first time I had seen such a large one with sliding doors. It ran along a whole wall. She opened it and I never, ever saw anything quite like it except maybe in a department store. Coats, dresses, shoes, and good Persian rugs were contained therein. I said to myself that it most likely all came from Jewish homes. I wondered if I should take this job, but I rationalized that those people from whom it was seized could never get it back. I selected a dark, green coat, made of a terrycloth-like material, with a hood attached, which would serve me well for the winter. As she gave me the coat, I suggested that she might possibly have my size shoes as well. Her shoe size was about a half size larger than mine. I received a pair of shoes as a bonus.

I went back and told the Loho family that I got the position, and they were all very happy. While I was away on the job interview, I was told that a woman had come by and asked for me. She said that she met her sister midway between Cracow and Chelm, where they went on business. She had brought a package of clothing for me from my mother in Chelm. This woman was Polish, definitely peasant looking. She asked for me by name, and left the address where I could pick up my package. I picked it up the next day. This visit of an honest-to-goodness Polish woman who asked for me by name definitely strengthened my claim to being a Pole.

It was urgent that I moved out of the Loho household soon. However, I could not start my new job just yet, and then the Christmas preparations intervened.

Just about a week prior to the holiday, I started to work at my new job. Twice a week, I cleaned the house. Mrs. Sierecki had left for Köln and her husband remained at home. This was the reason for the limitation of my services. In the meantime, I helped the Loho family with preparations and we celebrated Christmas together. I passed as a Catholic with flying colors because I knew all the appropriate ritual observances attendant upon the Christmas supper. We sang Christmas carols and we shared a pleasant Christmas Eve. I still have a photograph of that celebration. This was a very festive occasion in which we all participated, family and boarders. It was also tinged with sadness because many of us were far from home, some perhaps Jewish. There was a lot of reminiscing although I did very little talking about my family. A gentleman among us recalled leaving his wife and regretting the fact that he was unable to spend this time with her. We sang more Christmas songs and on the following day I took the children to church.

However, because of the neighbor's persistent threats, things became more tense. The Loho family urged me to expedite my departure. Not that they didn't want me, but they were afraid of the neighbors and of the possible repercussions.

The day after Christmas I rose to go to the home of Mr. Sierecki, my German employer. When I arrived, the house looked as if a cyclone had passed through. Glasses were strewn all over the place; the bathroom was in terrible condition; people must have become sick in there. The other rooms were in disarray. Mr. Sierecki was not home; I had a key to the apartment. In spite of my revulsion, I cleaned up the mess.

When I returned to the Lohos, I informed them that the next morning I would leave a little earlier in order for me to see Mr. Sierecki before he left for his office. I told Mr. Sierecki that it was most important that I move out of my present quarters. He tried to convince me that he could not really take me in; because his wife was still away and because he was alone, the neighbors would be sure to gossip. I realized that the real reason he did not want me there was that he arranged clandestine parties. While we were talking, he apologized for the appearance of the place the day before, and with a cryptic little smile said, "I hope you will keep it to yourself. Mrs. Sierecki is coming back next week and when she does, we will discuss the matter and you will move in."

I didn't promise to keep quiet, but I realized that it was not my business to disrupt their lives. Mrs. Sierecki returned a few days before New Year's Day, we met, and they decided that I could move in. The day after she came back from the visit with her parents in Köln, she tried to elicit from me some information about her husband's activities while she was away. She wanted to know whether he had remained faithful to her. I kept my composure and answered that I did not know of or see anything suspicious.

She added, "You didn't notice whether there were parties, if there were ladies . . . you are so stupid—don't you know how a bed looks when one or two people occupy it?"

I repeated that I saw nothing. Each time she spoke, I visualized the bathroom with all the filth, and the broken glasses on the floor. I insisted that I saw nothing. During that week she questioned me every day.

One day, while I was making the beds, I heard her call me rather impatiently, "Maria!" I wondered what could have happened in the kitchen.

As I walked through the door, she said, "Why didn't you tell me that you are Jewish?" I turned white, my blood must have rushed to my toes. "What's going on . . . what kind of an idea is that? You have seen my papers."

"Look, you are so different from all the maids that have worked for me. You must have seen a great deal during my absence yet you never told me that Werner had wild parties while I was gone."

I said, "What wild parties? I know nothing about such things."

She said "I know what happened because my next door neighbor told me that she saw girls coming and going, and that Werner arranged these socials."

"It is not my business to report any of these events to you."

She answered, "Well, my neighbor told me."

So I said, "If your neighbor wishes to tell you, she is in a different position than I am. He was nice to me when I came. In the beginning you told me that he would be the one who would refuse to hire me, but he did accept me. I have no reason to speak against him."

"It was a nice gesture on your part, but it also convinced me that you are not an ordinary maid. I am sorry, but I was curious and I went through all of your belongings because I knew you would deny it."

She had thoroughly examined my coat, including the lining. I also owned a large woolen muff in the lining of which she found two pictures, one of myself and my mother, and the other of me and a young man who lived nearby, both taken in the ghetto, both with the compulsory white armbands that were visible.

She had obviously ripped the lining and removed them, and now said, "You are lucky that it was I who found them; with anybody else it would have meant your immediate death. It is very foolish for you to carry such incriminating evidence, and I want you to burn these pictures." She lit the gas stove, "Here, take the two of them and burn them."

I refused, so she destroyed them. I was quite upset.

"Look, this is going to be your secret and mine. We will never tell my husband because if he finds out, he will not like it." It was at this time that she decided that I would be better off if I went to Germany to work for her parents in Köln. Soon thereafter she contacted her parents to see if they could provide me with an affidavit.

The Siereckis were planning a New Year's party in their home, and I moved in a day or two before New Year's Eve so I could help prepare for this event. In the package from Mrs. Dzwigaj's sister I found a little maroon dress with a white Peter Pan collar and dainty white cuffs, which suited me quite well for serving on New

Year's Eve. There were lots of German ladies and gentlemen at the party, all members of the SS. When I was finished serving, I asked to be excused. I entered the kitchen, which was small, and drew the curtain that covered the alcove. I prayed that I would not have to use the bathroom; there was only one. About an hour after I went to bed I heard some movement in the kitchen. I thought it might be Mr. or Mrs. Sierecki, but suddenly I caught sign of somebody approaching my alcove: it was a fat, drunken German. I really didn't know what to do at that moment, scream, or run. I had been smart enough to undress only partially. I just lay on the bed waiting for the guests to leave. The man was quite inebriated. I was able to push him away, and he fell like a sack of coal. Someone in the other room must have heard the commotion. Mr. Sierecki came in, berated the man, and dragged him from the kitchen. I was very scared. After a long time I finally fell asleep. The party ended in the early morning.

Early the next day I rose and started cleaning; there was the dining room to tidy up. The Siereckis were sleeping late. At midday Mrs. Sierecki left for the officers' club to attend a special dinner. Before she left, she asked if I would like to go to the back entrance of the club where a lot of food was available. She was not a homebody; she preferred to eat out whenever possible. I really didn't care to go because there was plenty of food left over from her party. But I finally went, carrying a little shopping bag. She emerged with small dishes containing puddings and other delicacies. I returned to their home and had my dinner. They had served roast piglet at the party. Mrs. Sierecki had asked me if I had thrown out the bones because she wanted no garbage kept in the house. I told her that I did not get rid of the bones because my friends the Lohos had a large dog and I thought that he would have a feast with those leftovers. I put them in bags and hung them outside the window on the little balcony.

On New Year's Day, I asked Mrs. Sierecki if I could visit my friends and take along the bones for their dog; she gave her permission. I went to call on the Lohos. They lived in the back section of the house. I quickly ran up to the first floor. The door had a glass window draped with curtains. I heard voices and saw people inside. The Lohos entertained all kinds of people in their home and I was so excited about all the good food I was bringing that I wasn't too alert. Without thinking, I opened the door and saw several Polish policemen inside. The entrance led straight into the kitchen, and rather than enter and place my package on the kitchen counter, I backed up, turned around, and ran. One of the policemen noticed that I was frightened. He chased me and that was my undoing. Obviously they were there because the neighbors had finally filed a report.

The police had a detailed description of me, the green coat, bleached blonde, etc. After the policeman caught up with me, they wanted to know why I ran away. I was devastated because I knew that once I was caught, I would have a hard time explaining my behavior, as well as my name change.

Chapter 10

ARREST AND IMPRISONMENT

THE POLICEMEN PLACED me under arrest. By a strange coincidence this was the very same station where I had reported my stolen papers when I returned from Zakopane. This happened the afternoon of New Year's Day, a holiday. The station was not fully manned. The man on duty was quite nasty. He noticed that when I claimed that I was robbed, I used a different name than the one I did now. He was extremely suspicious and decided to keep me overnight. In the evening, when everybody had left, I suggested that they call my German employer who I hoped would intervene on my behalf. Unfortunately, Mr. Sierecki was not at home. His wife answered. I told her that I had been picked up in the Lohos' home and that I was being detained at the police station, and could she help. She informed me that Werner was not home but that when he returned, she could talk with him and call back. In the meantime, she spoke with the arresting officer and verbally tried to throw her weight around. "You let her go; she works for me and I must have the food coupons she has. You had better send her home."

He explained that he was just a powerless employee who could not make such decisions. I was under arrest. The chief was not available because it was a holiday. She could call on the following day, or she could appear with her husband to intercede on my behalf. The policeman then handed me the phone and asked me to make our conversation short. Mrs. Sierecki's last words to me were a portent that she could not really do anything for me.

The following day I was once again subjected to an interrogation. This time my ordeal was much rougher. They screamed and threatened. They even attempted physical force, but I stood my ground and kept repeating, "I am not Jewish, I am not Jewish."

The chief said, "If you don't admit that you are a Jew, I am going to throw this typewriter at you."

I was very scared, and at that point, he dropped that large machine quite close to me. Luckily, it only hit my toes. He really only meant to frighten me. It hurt and as I screamed, he started hitting me again.

Finally I realized that there was more to come, so I confessed, "All right, I am Jewish. Leave me alone and send me wherever you have to. Just get it over with."

After that, they sent me to a cell-like room for a time. I didn't hear from any-one until the late afternoon. Then I was recalled by the police chief. He delivered a long speech and ended with a suggestion. "Now that I know you are Jewish, I am going to help you." I was not sure what he meant, and he explained that this building has an upper floor with several rooms used by policemen on the night shift. He offered to hide me in one of these rooms. He tried to sound sincere, but my gut reaction was not to trust him. I asked what was in it for him. Well, the guys come here on occasion and they sleep over. At times they are on a twenty-four-hour tour of duty and they can't go home. . . .

He wasn't too explicit, but he kept talking about those tired and overworked officers and I knew exactly what he meant. I asked him if he had to have an an-swer immediately and he said of course. I thought very quickly and remembered what my mother had advised: if this was going to save my life, I should give them what they wanted. On the other hand, I asked myself, how long could they keep me upstairs? How secret could it be if more than one person knew? From my early days I had been taught that confidential matters should remain the property of only one person. I was scared and did not know what my alternative was, but I knew intuitively that this was not a good plan. Or maybe I was just too afraid.

I said, "No, I don't want to enter into that kind of agreement." I knew that they would soon tire of it. I was also aware that some Poles were drunkards and one of them when inebriated could hurt me. I refused his thinly veiled proposition.

"This means that you are going to be turned over to the Gestapo and you will be in their custody."

Eventually the Polish police decided to send me to Montelupich, which was the largest and most notorious jail in Cracow. Prior to the actual transfer I asked them to call the Lohos who lived nearby and had many friends in the precinct. The chief called them. The evening before I was scheduled to leave, the grandmother, the mother, and the two children visited me. The little boy couldn't understand why I was being detained, and I don't think they were able to explain all the whys and wherefores of my situation to him. They all appeared rather somber. The young boy offered me some food from his supper and the grandmother brought me a cup of hot coffee and something sweet. They visited with me for about half an hour. When they left, I was returned to my cell.

It took about two days before all paperwork was satisfactorily completed. I was asked to speak with the chief a few more times. Whenever I had an opportunity to speak with him, I was kept in the waiting room on the ground floor. To avoid talking with anyone else, I occupied myself with looking out of the barred window that faced a narrow barren backyard. Once, I remember seeing a little bird perched on the outside ledge. I distinctly recall the sadness that enveloped me, as I watched that little creature flittering about. The cliche, "free as a bird" came to my mind, and with it the forlorn awareness that I had just lost my freedom forever. I wished I were dead. I was quite sure that I would soon be transferred to the main prison where I would probably be shot, as this was the usual procedure. Once a Jew was caught, he might be killed on the spot. An overwhelming feeling of hopelessness and desolation came over me and did not leave me for months.

The following morning a young Polish policeman was assigned to walk me to Montelupich. As we walked along the street, I asked him to let me go. He responded that, as part of the police force, he was trained to scrupulously obey the law and he was not about to break it now. I said, "We are on a very crowded street, and I am not handcuffed." He hesitated and I thought that if I really wanted to escape, he would probably allow me. I was spent, had no money and no place to go. I had been befriended by a Polish family who treated me as one of their own, but the inhabitants of the entire back courtyard were already aware that I had been arrested. So I really couldn't return to them. I would not go back to that lady who had taken me in, not after I admitted to the police that I was a Jew. Suddenly I felt very tired and told him that I was just testing him, and to do what we had to do to get it over with. He then said that he did not think the Germans were going to shoot me because there were new orders revising the old procedures. Allegedly, the Germans' supply of ammunition was low and so bullets should not be wasted on Jews. He added that the Germans would probably not liquidate individual Jews but would hold the apprehended ones in prison, and punish them en masse.

He led me to the prison office on the fifth floor. I was upset that there were so many Polish clerks. There weren't many Germans present. The Poles acted in a very haughty and deprecating manner.

They asked me all kinds of questions to which I responded: "Why are you asking me these stupid questions? I have already admitted my culpability to the accusations." Then I started to tease them, since I had nothing to lose at the time. I castigated them for their subservience to their oppressors and asked what they expect would happen to them when all the Jews were gone. I was quite orally aggressive because I was angry. I warned them that as soon as the Germans exterminated the Jews, they would use the Poles as scapegoats. They ordered me to shut up.

After I was registered they sent me down to a dungeon-like room. It was a very large place and crammed with people. Among them were young women who appeared to be prostitutes. Men were sitting on the other side of the room. It resembled a holding pen plagued by a variety of insects. I was afraid to sit, but I couldn't stand all night. The guard informed us that on the next day they would dispose of us in one way or another and we would all receive our future assignments.

We were served the slop they called food by a nun. I couldn't eat it. I was quite depressed. At this time I regretted that they had not shot me. I just couldn't sit and wait for something to happen.

The next morning a guard escorted me to the main investigation room. I wanted to know why I was going back to be questioned by the inept Poles. I was told that I was to report to the main office for the Gestapo interrogation. They wanted to know whether I received any help from any organization in securing my papers and birth certificate. They knew that many organizations, for a fee, falsified documents. When I entered, I was told to sit and wait in the outer area until I was called. On the walls hung posters depicting Hitler winning the war and stepping on the Russians. They were very colorful and there were many of them.

I sat there for some time, and then Mr. and Mrs. Sierecki walked in through the side door. He was attired in his SS regalia and she was wearing my beautiful fur coat. He entered the waiting room, ostensibly attracted by the colorful posters. He walked through the room studying them intently. He didn't approach me directly but he moved in my direction. He finally stopped to read the poster behind me. As he was pretending to appreciate it, he whispered to me that he was very sorry that I admitted to being Jewish. He explained that if I had confessed to killing somebody, or that I had committed the most heinous of crimes, he could probably have saved me. He could have shipped me out or made some sort of plea-bargaining arrangement. But the fact that I had admitted to being a Jew made it necessary for him to completely disassociate himself from me because to do otherwise would undoubtedly mean the loss of his job.

He said, "When you are being interrogated, and you see us playing along with the Gestapo chief, we are doing so only because we have to." I couldn't have cared less. I wasn't angry or upset. I was completely numb.

When I walked into the huge room, the SS chief asked me all sorts of questions. Mrs. Sierecki sat at the other end of the table and together with her husband just listened. Mr. Sierecki was asked whether his wife and he knew I was Jewish, how they found out, and why they hired me. They answered very briefly that they didn't know, that they had checked me out, that I had brought a birth certificate and everything seemed in order. So the only query left was why, if my original paper stipulated that it was valid for eight weeks only, and as the eight-week period had already passed, why had he done nothing? Mr. Sierecki said it had slipped his mind. I was a good person (and this was the only time he said this). They had employed many maids who robbed them and did all kinds of things in their house. He definitely had no reason to suspect anything as I performed my duties well and I was clean. He maintained that I was intelligent, read books, and it never occurred to him to question me since I assured him that I was in the process of getting new papers. He added that I was also a good companion for his wife. Then followed the official exchange. I gave the food ration coupons to the Gestapo man who in turn let Mrs. Sierecki have them. When he handed them to her, tears were streaming down her face. He bawled her out . . . what kind of a foolishness was it to cry about one Jew. At that time she also affirmed that I was different in a positive way from the other girls who had worked for her and that she suspected nothing.

At that point Mr. Sierecki asked, "What do you think will happen to her now?"

The chief replied, "Well, we don't have too many of them here, but we do have a couple and we decided that since Cracow will be Judenrein very shortly, we will send them to the ghetto there."

"Will she be working like the others?" he asked.

"No, we will remand her to the Cracow ghetto jail."

All this interchange was conducted in front of me as if I were not present.

After the hearing, when we returned to the same waiting room with the benches, a rather handsome young man attired in a Jewish police uniform was waiting for me. Apparently they had sent a horsedrawn two-wheeled, two-seater carriage to convey me. At this time the Siereckis walked out and noticed the policeman. Outside of the hearing room, Mr. Sierecki became a little more active; he had been very calm inside. Now he approached the policeman asking, "I understand that you are going to transfer her into the ghetto prison. Do they treat them well in there?"

He was told, "Of course; it is a Jewish prison and this is a Jew."

Mr. Sierecki said, "Well, make sure she is treated well!"

We rode in the carriage. The officer drove and I sat next to him. He wanted to know what kind of a person I was to induce this German to intercede on my behalf. Mr. Sierecki had taken a risk in doing that in front of the Poles but I suppose that he wasn't too concerned about it; he had spoken in German.

I said: "I don't know what kind of a person I am—I am a Jew living outside of the ghetto, trying to save my life."

When I arrived at the ghetto prison, I discovered that among the inmates were many more people like me.

Some of them had false documents and some even had valid ones. I learned that most of them were betrayed by Poles. The Germans usually did not recognize them. They could have survived, but there were many Poles who felt it was their duty to turn in Jews. Some of these unfortunates had also walked into traps, just as I did. We spent another two weeks in that jail.

The prison food wasn't bad. Most of it consisted of a variety of soups. We were not required to work. Once or twice a day they would take us out to the yard to walk. The rest of the time we sat around talking, trading stories with each other and waiting. I told them that we were waiting because there would be a Judenrein campaign soon and we were selected to leave with the transport of the Cracow ghetto. That is exactly what happened. On March 13, 1943, there was Judenrein. They liquidated the Cracow ghetto.

Coat of arms of the city of Chelm, Poland.

Felicia Berland, age 5, and
her mother Sara. Krycica,
Poland, 1925

Abraham and Sara Berland. Chelm, 1924

May Day parade, Chelm, May 1, 1930. Abe Berland (father) is the flag bearer.

Berland house in process of being built. Living quarters upstairs, bakery downstairs. Father in center door; mother and builder in left window. Chelm, 1931

Felicia and parents. Chelm, 1933

Abraham, Sara, and Felicia Berland, maternal grandmother (Chaya Rachel Hilf), and visiting cousin Hela. Chelm, 1933

Close school friends, nicknamed the Quintumvirate. Sitting: Kazia, Eva, Henia, Marysia. Standing: Felicia (Felka). Chelm, 1933

Rosie and Hershel, mother's cousins who were hosts to Felicia and parents in Warsaw during 1938 and until September 1939. Warsaw, mid-1920s

Clockwise from top: Genia and
Felicia in gimnazium wearing
school uniform hats. Chelm, 1932;
Felicia and two friends walking
home from school in uniform.
Chelm, 1934; Felicia and mother,
after graduation. Felicia wearing
custom-made clothes and first
high heels. Chelm, June 1938;
Sara Berland and her cousin
Rosie, with whom Sara and
Felicia spent time in Warsaw.
Chelm, 1937

Clockwise from left: Felicia Berland. Chelm, 1936; Paternal grandmother, Hanna Rachel Berland. Chelm, 1937; Grave of paternal grandfather, Pinchas, son of Arieh, who died in 1917 or earlier. The engraving is in the form of an acrostic, with the first letter of each line spelling out the name. Front from left: Ethel Berland Lis, Grandmother Berland, Chavala Berland Globen, Sara Berland Hilf, Israel Lis. Back from left: Yankiel Berland, Abraham Berland, Abram Globen, David Grinwald. Chelm, 1937

Loho family. Sitting from left: Jadzia, Mrs. Loho, Felicia aka Maria Klimczak. Standing from left: Guest-boarder, Boleslawa Urbancyzk, Andrew, Mr. Loho. Cracow, Christmas 1942

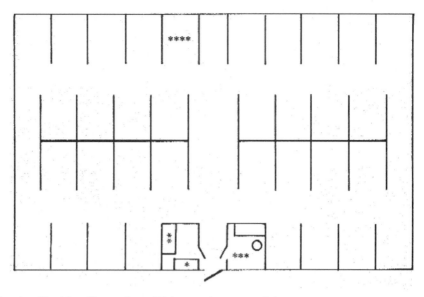

Sketch of inside of barracks at Birkenau (not to scale):
  * Blockälteste's bed
  ** Bunk bed for Veträterin and Schreiberin
  *** Kammerstube: Storage room with long worktable, bench, and chair.
      In this room, clothing was stored, bread was cut.
  **** A typical stall had three levels, each sleeping 10 – 12 prisoners, head to foot
      (like sardines in a can). Prisoners kept their clothing under the mattress
      when they slept, to avoid theft. A typical barracks unit housed approxi-
      mately one thousand prisoners.

Loho grandchildren, Andrew
and Jadwiga Urbanczyk.
Cracow, 1942

Felicia and two prewar friends, Guta and Blumka. The army and air force lieutenants are Jewish young men who served in the Polish army after the Russians pushed Hitler back. Lodz, 1945

Masza (who hosted Felicia in Chelm in 1945) and her husband. Chelm, 1945

A gathering with friends the day before departure for Sweden. Paula and Herman are on the left. Lodz, 1946

Felicia and Fini, her roommate in Sweden. Strotop, Sweden, 1946

Clockwise from top: Zosia and Gerszon, students at the University in Stockholm. Center is Misza, Gerszon's brother. Zosia was a good friend of Felicia's at Auschwitz. They met again in Sweden. She now lives in Sweden and Israel, spending six months of the year in each country. Stockholm, 1946; Paula and Herman, friends with whom Felicia lived in Lodz, 1945; Felicia and Blumka, who invited Felicia to live with her in Lodz. Blumka survived the war as an Aryan. She now lives in Israel. Lodz, 1946

Judith, her husband, and their children. They now live in Israel. Natanya, Israel, 1947

Felicia and friends from Auschwitz: Hilda, her Blockälteste, and Magda, the Verträterin. This photo was taken the day before Felicia's departure for the United States. Stockholm, July 1948

ADDRESS
DISTRICT SUPERINTENDENT
ATLANTIC DISTRICT

IN YOUR REPLY REFER TO
NO. B. 83306
IMMIGRATION
BRANCH

CANADA

DEPARTMENT
OF
MINES AND RESOURCES

Ottawa, May 28, 1948.

Dear Sir:-

     With reference to your application for the admission to Canada of your sister, Felicia Berland,

presently residing at Glasmalerwagen, Enskede, Stockholm, Sweden,

this is to advise that the settlement arrangements for the reception of the above-named are considered satisfactory and it will be in order for her to make application in person to the Canadian Visa Officer at The Canadian Legation, Stockholm, Sweden.

     Provided the proposed immigrant is of good character, in possession of travel document establishing identity,

can pass medical examination and otherwise comply with our requirements, visa for Canada will be granted.

     This letter should be sent to the above-named for presentation to the Canadian Visa Officer indicated for the purpose of identification.

     The necessary advice is going forward to the Visa Officer overseas by surface mail which takes from three to four weeks to arrive and the proposed immigrant should therefore refrain from getting in touch with said Officer until sufficient time has elapsed for our advice to reach him.

     Yours very truly,

Nathan Berliner, Esq.,
206 Villeneuve St. W.,
Montreal, P.Q.

H. U. McCrum,
10.   District Superintendent.

Letter permitting Felicia to emigrate to Canada.

Abraham Berland, after his
arrival in New York, 1942.

This is the Gimnazium Stefana Czarnieckiego that Felicia attended.
Chelm, 1991

The former Berland home in Chelm, as it appeared in 1991.

Graffiti on a wall in Chelm says: "JEWS, GET YOURSELVES OUT OF POLAND AND
OUT OF TELEVISION!" Please note that in 1991 there were no Jews in Chelm.

Chapter 11

TRUCKED TO AUSCHWITZ-BIRKENAU[12]

I WAS TWENTY-THREE years old at the time. Early that day we heard noises coming from the ghetto. The sounds were quite unusual. We heard the Germans command, *"Raus, raus."* We heard the screams of families that were separated and those of children crying for their parents. We, the prisoners, were the last ones to go. When the entire ghetto had supposedly been cleared out, we were called. There were twenty-four of us. We were assembled in size place and led to the military trucks.

I was the smallest, so I was the last to be loaded. When my turn came to get on the truck, it seemed completely filled. The Germans pushed me in with the butts of their guns and there was no room to place my feet. I was afraid that when the flat board was closed I would be hurt. I pleaded with the occupants to move back, to give me a little space. But everybody was so frightened and stiff that they seemed to be fixed in place, and no one moved. I grabbed the upper frame that held the canvas covering and hung on to it, pulling my feet up to avoid getting hurt. The backboard was finally secured and the truck was closed. It was pitch dark inside and as the German faces disappeared, everyone relaxed somehow. I felt a shifting of the bodies, which permitted me to step down onto the floor. I cried for awhile; nobody said anything. Suddenly, from somewhere in the front of the truck, somebody suggested that we rip the covering and make a run for it. He was told to keep quiet. The convoy started to move. Since I was at the very end, I was able to peek through the cracks in the cover and to notice that we were surrounded by motorcycles and cars, and guarded like precious cargo.

We moved out of the city rather slowly. The streets, from what we could see, were completely deserted. After about ten minutes, somebody spoke up again

---

12. Birkenau was a satellite of the main camp at Auschwitz. The distance between the two was about three kilometers. Auschwitz housed most of the administrative offices, in addition to prisoners and laboratories for human experiments. Birkenau had the gas chambers, the ovens, and the largest number of prisoners. Most reference books and guide books refer to Birkenau as Auschwitz II. Here I use the names interchangeably.

from the other end of the truck; "We know where we are going . . . we are not going to be led like docile animals to slaughter . . . let's do something . . . let's run." There was a great deal of arguing, but the consensus was that we were not going to run too far. There still was a group of people in the truck who tried to stop the activists from talking and raising false hopes. They felt that even if we did succeed momentarily, the Poles would inform on us. The speaker insisted, "When we get out of the city, let's try to think of something to do." There was silence for awhile; as we moved out of Cracow and started to approach open spaces, the discussion continued in a whisper, for fear of being overheard by the Germans.

Eventually they did hear. They stopped the truck. Somebody entered and began screaming at us. It was very interesting. When the German entered the truck, everyone moved towards the front, leaving an empty aisle at the back. I stood there and wondered. How did it happen that there had been no room when I was trying to get in and now suddenly everybody managed to squeeze to the front of the truck?

Two German soldiers came up to yell at us and the minute they left, the man who was promoting the escape attempt insisted that we must try to escape. We were canvassed to learn who had a sharp instrument that we could use to rip the canvas cover. Someone found a small pair of manicure scissors, which were used to cut a hole in the cover. I wasn't involved in this. I wasn't taking the risk. I was too desolate, too exhausted. I knew I couldn't run. But some of the young people were really determined to escape. After the canvas was ripped apart, people started jumping out of the truck. Not too many, maybe five or six. Of course the Germans immediately began shooting at them. We stayed inside because we knew that the Germans would punish all of us if anyone jumped.

As I looked out, I saw that two or three people were killed or wounded. Some were able to run far enough away to avoid being shot. The woman who ripped the canvas fell first. I could see that she was not shot, but feigned being hit. Our truck was stopped and boarded by the Germans who told us that, as punishment for the attempt to escape, we would be executed as soon as we arrived at Auschwitz. Huddled together we traveled for what seemed like an eternity. Even though perhaps ten people at most leaped from the transport, it looked as if half the truck was empty, because we held to each other so tightly.

Ours had been the last truck in the convoy of Jews from the Cracow ghetto. After the aborted escape attempt, our truck rejoined the convoy. However, because of the incident, our truck was diverted to Auschwitz, while the rest proceeded directly to Birkenau. At Auschwitz, our punishment was to be decided.

They unloaded the truck and placed us facing the wall of a red brick building.

We stood there, waiting for the end. Again, it seemed like an eternity; I don't know how long it lasted. We didn't hear guns being loaded; we just stood holding our breaths. We stood there for an unconscionably long time, unable to hear them discussing our fate. One of the highest ranking German officers told us that he was ordered to shoot us. Fortunately, someone came down and told the SS men not to shoot us. Instead, we were to go to Birkenau.

They put us back on the truck and tried to mend the torn cover so that we would be unable to see where we were going. They were only partially successful and we could look outside. It was a beautiful sunny day. We saw fragments of the cloudless blue sky. Eventually we arrived at the infamous ramp in Birkenau. The SS men arrived, screaming and barking orders. They rushed us off the truck. We formed a small group in a large assemblage from Cracow. Again, they were at a loss to know what to do with us. We were prisoners who were sentenced to death, but something else was in store for us. The protocols were so ridiculous that the man in charge had to inquire from a number of commandants to learn our destination and fate.

We joined an entire group of disabled people on crutches, many who were sick, and many children: we looked quite different from the people around us. We were better dressed, healthier and younger, and we knew immediately that we were condemned to the gas chambers. It seemed inconceivable to me that this was the last day of my life and the last time I would see the sun. I made a comment to that effect. One of the women with whom I had become friendly in the ghetto prison admonished me for being overly dramatic and felt that I was unduly concerned with the sky and the sun. She advised that I was better off making peace with myself, praying to God and asking for his forgiveness. Finally we were ordered to move to the right, in the direction of the gas chambers and crematoria, though the people who were young and looked healthier went to the other side.

On our way to the crematorium, we caught a glimpse of the camp on our left. We saw the tall electrified wire fences, and people moving about, trying to work, but watching us at the same time. They resembled shadows from another world. They were all women, wearing rags. The Germans who were patrolling the camp kept yelling at the women to keep away from the fence. A ditch separated the actual camp ground and the fences. They were too far away for us to see clearly but we caught a glimpse of those emaciated shadows moving at an extremely slow pace. Here we were, unable to proceed faster because of the group's infirmities. There were Germans on either side of us with dogs and with guns.

The woman next to me asked why we had not escaped when we had the chance and I said that if we had run away we probably would be dead now. She remarked that we didn't miss anything because we still could flee towards the electric wire to die of our own will and not as sheep being led to slaughter. We continued with our philosophical discussions. I agreed with her that we should express some opposition. We both laughed because no one could care less whether or not we took a stand to profess our defiance.

As we crawled along, we noticed a young SS man coming toward us from the direction of the crematorium on a motorcycle. One of the young women in our group jumped out of formation and in front of his cycle. He could easily have run her down, but he applied his brakes quickly and effectively, avoiding serious injury to the girl, or even death. The Germans screamed and pointed their guns at the woman. The officer on the motorcycle ordered them to stop yelling. He was taken by surprise and offered his observation and disbelief that the Jew was brave enough to risk her life.

The girl started to talk very hurriedly, informing him that she was not Jewish, that she was caught right outside of the ghetto during the Judenrein action. The ghetto was divided into two parts, with a main street running through the center. She said that she was on her way to work and did not live far from the ghetto fence and while the Jews were being seized, she was stupidly caught up in the roundup. She told him a story that didn't make much sense to us, and probably not to him either, but he was so impressed with the risk that this young lady took that he just stood there listening and looking at her. To me, he appeared very tall, resembling all of his compatriots. He was dressed immaculately and impressively. He wore highly polished tall riding boots; he held a whip in his hand.

After she finished her story, he said, "All right, what can you do?" She said that she was a dental technician. He told her that he could use her in the camp and that she could go back. He added that he believed her when she maintained that she did not belong with this group.

As soon as we saw that she was not going to return, all of us jumped out of formation and crowded around him. Everyone had a different tale to tell; all insisted that we were not Jewish. He smiled, and at times ridiculed and yelled at us. We all tried to convince him that we looked so different from the people around us. We were all well-dressed, unlike the ghetto inhabitants. We looked healthier. He kept shaking his head in disbelief. He then asked everyone to tell him what we could offer that might be useful in the camp. All professed membership in various professions or occupations.

There were twenty-four of us. He studied us intently but I don't know whether he really listened. I told him that I was a seamstress and a very skillful knitter. He asked me how old I was. I added about three years to my age. He looked at me, shook his head and said, "Ya, I guess we could find something for you to do in camp."

Finally he got to the last person who was much taller than I and perhaps a bit more mature than all of us. He asked for her profession and I believe she said nursing. He looked at her and thought for a while. She was wearing a very bright red kerchief over her hair. With his whip he moved the kerchief away from her temples. He found that although she was a young woman, she was completely gray, prematurely so. He looked at her once more and said: "Well, I guess you've lived long enough; you are all gray, you may join the rest." She was the only one who was told to rejoin the people who were selected for the crematorium. In the meantime, the people started to move, and we were left standing on the side. The woman pleaded with him: she cried bitterly, but he wouldn't listen, and told the guards to take her back.

The twenty-three of us once again lined up in a formation of five in a row. He didn't get back on the motorcycle; he just rolled the bike next to us and took us all the way back to the selection ramp and to the commandant of the camp. He left us standing on the side, several feet away and went back to speak with the camp *Kommandant*. Apparently, from what we heard him say in German, he argued that it was wrong to send such healthy young women to the gas chamber. He continued that there were many tasks we could perform in camp. I learned later that the two were not the best of friends, but they finally agreed to admit us to the camp. Then, for the first time, I noticed the arched gates over which hung the emblazoned slogan *Arbeit Macht Frei*.[13] We were all thinking about how free we were going to be there, but we were grateful. And thankful. We were aware that our lives were spared at this particular time, and that there would be hard times ahead, but we did have another chance.

---

13. Work makes one free.

Chapter 12

INITIATION AT AUSCHWITZ-BIRKENAU

THE FACT THAT I have difficulties in recalling my first impressions of entering Auschwitz seems quite significant to me. I believe that this was so painful that it was unconsciously repressed, and recalling it becomes a real problem.

The skies that appeared so lovely, blue, and sunny when we were in the trucks on the way to Birkenau, suddenly became overcast with black clouds. The stench was intolerable. Suddenly the outline of the chimneys came into focus and we saw the billowing black smoke and flames emanating from them.

The sense of exhilaration induced by the last minute reprieve from the crematorium and our return to the camp was quickly dissipated because we realized that even though our lives were spared, it was only a temporary respite.

As we marched in, the twenty-three of us and one SS guard, we attracted a group of inmates who eagerly rushed towards us asking where we came from. Our group had just come from Cracow, but we all hailed from different cities. Initially we said that we came from Cracow; as they came near, each of us told the names of our hometowns, and they asked, "Did you know this one?" "Did you see that one?" They plied us with questions. "What do you hear about the progress of the war? What is happening on the outside?"

We were eventually separated from the old inmates and admitted to temporary quarters. We remained there overnight. As we woke up the next morning we noted that the sky over the camp was still ominously dark and the air continued to reek indescribably. That stench stayed with me for years after I left Auschwitz and returned to Poland where the many bombed out houses seemed to be permeated with a similarly putrid odor.

It was late in the day. They placed us all into temporary barracks. Someone, a very ugly looking German, came in to talk with us and said that nothing would be done for us that day. Somebody would probably come in the next day and talk with us about how we managed to get into the camp. If we lied about not being

Jewish, they had ways of confirming our stories. In the meantime, we realized that they no longer contemplated killing us. We were informed again that they had a method of ascertaining whether we were telling the truth. The next day someone would arrive to handle the registration. For that entire afternoon and evening, we talked with each other. All of us were tense trying to decide whether we should admit to being Jewish or continue to insist that we are Aryan.

The following morning, March 14, 1943, they assembled us again and brought us to the bathhouses where we were prepared for registration, cleaning, and delousing. After we entered, we were led into a medium-sized room. There, behind a table, sat a rather important looking SS man. Next to him was the ugly guard who had addressed us when we first entered the camp. We were told to line up and await our turn. When we came face to face with the two Germans, we were asked to give our names, birth dates, and most important, our race. That was when we had to make our dreaded decision. The ugly German—he was a sergeant, I believe—roared like an animal, screaming, and exhorting us not to lie about not being Jewish. He assured us that the authorities knew all about our racial antecedents, and that we might have fooled the other interrogator because he was stupid.

It was interesting that as we came closer to the registration and tattooing, we started to split halfway about our race. Many of the girls continued to insist that they were Polish and that they came with the Cracow ghetto group by mistake. The rest of us admitted to being Jewish.

My own thinking was that the apparatus for registering was a farce despite the elaborate precision they employed, yet on some level I hoped that those records would survive.

From the few letters that came through to us from my father during the war, I knew that he had to leave La Paz, Bolivia, because he could not tolerate the high altitude. Unable to immigrate to the United States, he moved to Panama from where his brothers in New York were able to arrange (by Act of Congress) for my father to go to the United States. This was at about the time the United States entered World War II. I hoped that this elaborate registration would enable my father to locate me, even after my death. I didn't want to perish in Auschwitz under an assumed name.

I registered as a Jew, I was tattooed on the outside of my left forearm with my number 38307,[14] and a triangle directly below the number. All tattooing was done

---

14. Numbers for prisoners were distributed in series of 100,000. In the first group of 100,000, Jews were identified by the triangle under the number, which was tattooed on the outside of the left forearm. Later tattoos were on the inside of the left forearm. The letter A with no triangle preceded the numbers in the next 100,000, then B, then C, for Jewish prisoners. German prisoners had numbers, but no tattoos. Poles, Serbs, Gypsies, and others had tattoos without triangles or letters. The triangle and/or the letters A, B, C, etc., distinguished the Jewish prisoners.

by prisoners. After we received our numbers, we were told to undress and to leave our clothing on the floor.

They herded us into a large room containing two long tables and a couple of prisoners. We lined up to be shaved. After they shaved our heads, they shaved our pubic areas and our underarms. Even though the barbers were prisoners, they were quite rough. The German SS men who were watching the procedures from the sides crowded around the tables where the pubic areas were being shaved. They all joked about what they saw. Before I left Chelm, I was a bleached blonde. When I was arrested, I had no opportunity to retouch my hair, so I was a partial platinum blonde, with the dark roots already visible. When my turn came, the SS guards jokingly remarked, here comes the blonde with a black "past," because my pubic area was dark. They enjoyed watching and instructing the barber-prisoners, pointing out that there was a hair left here or there. It was terribly humiliating. But it was, I know, fortunately different for us because we were spared the gas chamber. We already hoped that perhaps we might survive. We were so happy to be there, and even to be processed, that we almost didn't mind it. In our own way, we experienced a simultaneous sense of depression and elation.

Once they finished shaving us, we were herded into a little steam room, and as we entered, one after another, we became hysterical with laughter. We had spent a number of days in prison in rather close proximity. Without our hair, we just couldn't recognize each other and we had to identify ourselves by name. I think this was the first time that we felt a true emotional release of accumulated tension. This hysterical laughter brought us back to a new reality. The prisoners who were supervising the process came into the steam room to find out what was happening, because it was so unusual to hear us laughing so boisterously, while others usually wept so hopelessly.

After we sat there for awhile, they shoved us out of this hot steam room into another huge area where shower heads were in the ceiling, and the cement floor was ice cold. After the heat, the freezing cold water showered upon us and we started to scream. I noticed that the woman who was in charge of the proceedings wore black leather gloves. I wondered why this was necessary, but I soon learned that the impact of leather on a wet body can intensify the pain manyfold. She kept smacking and ordering us to keep quiet while we remained standing. She told us to wash properly because it was important that we stay clean. We received pieces of soap that were as abrasive as limestone. After a few seconds the showers were turned off to allow us to soap ourselves. After a few minutes the showers were turned on again but not long enough to totally remove the soap.

After the shower, they sent us into another room where we lined up to receive clothing. Several prisoners sat in front of tables distributing various items of apparel. I learned that Birkenau was once a POW camp for Polish and Russian soldiers. The clothing we received once belonged to those inmates. When my turn came, I got a pair of huge pants without a single button. I needed something to hold them up. I approached the lady with the leather gloves, and in my very best, classical German, asked her whether I could please have a piece of rope. She asked if I wanted to hang myself. "No, I just want to tie my pants." Instead of the rope, I received a smarting smack in my face. I toppled over. A fellow prisoner picked me up and said, "We will find a piece of string; just try to hold your pants up until we get to the corner." It turned out that she had been given a pair of very small pants, and since she was bigger than I, they were much too small for her. We quickly exchanged.

We learned very quickly to be independent, and not to ask any questions, to avoid any contact with authority if possible. We then walked over to a pile of shoes. This time I received laced ones. One was all right, the other one was small because it had shrunk in the steaming containers used for delousing. Now there I was with one shoe I couldn't get into. Oh yes, this was where we got the string: the two shoes were tied together with it. The woman prisoner who was in charge of distributing the shoes was a bit more sympathetic and when she noticed my dilemma, she came over to me and pretended to be rough. She screamed, and grabbing me, said: "What are you doing with those shoes? They are for someone else." She put them away and gave me another pair. Now I had no problems because my feet were so small that any pair would fit. Finally, we dressed in our "gorgeous" outfits, which elicited a great deal of laughter because we really looked ridiculous.

After the admitting process was completed we were led to special barracks and told that we would be quarantined for two weeks. To me it seemed like a charade because the camp internees looked much worse than we did. We just couldn't understand why we had to be quarantined while other sickly looking people were at large. They explained that since we were newly arrived from the outside world, there was a good possibility that we might be germ carriers.

For the next two weeks, we were confined to barracks. They fed us and let us out a couple of times a day to walk around the barracks.

Chapter 13

QUARANTINE AT
AUSCHWITZ-BIRKENAU

THE CAMP WAS DIVIDED into two parts by a large central road that extended from one end to the other. On one side of the road were many identical looking brick barracks, the rows of which were arranged in a geometrical pattern all facing the road. On the other side were differently planned barracks. We later learned that some of these quarters on the other side housed a hospital, the sauna, and some offices. At the time of our arrival there existed only one woman's camp at Birkenau.[15]

Each of the barracks housed about 1,000 women. The interior was divided into stalls, resembling those used for horses. Wooden planks divided each stall into three berths. There was never enough air. Twelve of us were jammed into one of these berths. We were forced to sleep six one way and six the other. We were packed in like sardines. At night, when one turned, the rest also had to turn. We received what they called straw mattresses; these were simply potato sacks filled with straw. After a couple of weeks, the straw became very flat and extremely thin. If people in your berth became ill and weak and couldn't manage to get to the bathroom in time, it was impossible to sleep on the mattress.

During the first two weeks when we did not have to report for work, we were well and still strong, and we managed. We even joked about it all. It was really gallows humor.

As a rule, the boards were weak. Quite frequently they would collapse and we would fall to the berth below. As we became more familiar with camp life, and were transferred to different barracks, we tried to avoid the middle berth.

When we received our first portion of soup while waiting to be processed, it took a long time, and we were very hungry. The soup had a very peculiar odor and contained chunks of something that looked like some sort of meat. It was brown or gray in color. Included also were parts of what could have been rotting sugar beets. One cynical member of our group, who was obviously surprised to

---

15. Birkenau had men's camps, women's camps, and Gypsy camps. When I arrived, there was only one women's camp there.

find pieces of meat in the soup, jokingly suggested that those were pieces of flesh of recently cremated prisoners. Though we were all quite hungry, we refused to eat the soup. But the old prisoners standing by were only too willing to take the food off our hands. I don't think that I ate soup for the first six months of my internment. Each time I attempted it, I choked.

We were each given a bowl when we entered the camp and we had to be very careful not to lose it as we could not get replacements. After awhile, we learned that each of us had to find, steal, or buy another similar bowl because we would use one for food and the other as a convenient substitute for the latrine at night. We joked about this arrangement, calling them a *pishka* and a *pushka*. Almost everyone owned two bowls.

When we were ordered to take a shower, we were rushed through very quickly. To maintain some semblance of cleanliness, we often used the so-called coffee, really an awful brew, for drinking and washing.

Despite our serious attempts to keep clean, we waged a losing battle against the lice in our clothing even though our apparel was deloused regularly. No matter how often we changed, whatever we wore was invariably full of lice. On Sunday afternoons, if and when we were free, we would sit on our beds and delouse each other—like monkeys.

I recall that I had to go to the bathroom. I was afraid to ask because we had learned from experience that when you ask, you are beaten. It was an emergency, and I didn't want to soil myself. I asked the lady who appeared to be in charge where to go, and she told me that outside was a wheelbarrow and I could use that if I wanted.

It was a memorable experience because, as I stepped out, I noticed that a few steps from the wheelbarrow two male prisoners were making some repairs. As soon as I saw them, I went back inside, but I still had to go and didn't know what to do. Finally one of the working men said, "Don't be bashful, if you've got to go, you've got to go; we will turn around, if that is the way it must be. You have no choice and we will not look."

This was reassuring. In the meantime, while I was tending to my needs, he asked me where I came from, when, and what was happening on the outside. Someone inside heard us talk; the woman in charge of the barracks yelled at me. However, before she interrupted us, we had some conversation while his back was turned. It was quite an experience, degrading and dehumanizing.

Very early we learned to ration our bread rations. We divided our bread into three portions, so that we could eat three times a day. Some devoured their entire allotment immediately and were desperately hungry at the end of the day. We always tried to get a full bowl of whatever they dished out, to fill our stomachs.

Soon after we arrived in camp we learned that Barracks Number 25 should be avoided. It was a holding place for those selected for the gas chamber. Jewish prisoners who were sick, unable to work, or otherwise considered unfit were kept there until a large group was assembled. Only large groups of prisoners were sent to be gassed.

During the quarantine period I formed a close relationship with one of the women from the Cracow ghetto prison. Her name was Judith. We would call her Juditka or Palestinka. She came to Poland from Palestine in August of 1939, a month before the war started. She was married and her husband had remained at home. She dreamt that her mother in Poland was very ill, so she returned to visit her. Mother was terminally ill and Judith arrived in time for a last farewell. Her mother died a day or two later. After this happened, Judith was unable to go back to Palestine because the war had started. We were close throughout our stay in the camp, but, at the end, we were separated. She ended up in Bergen-Belsen. Her husband was serving with the British RAF and, at the war's end, when they entered Bergen-Belsen, he found her there and took her home. I saw her in Israel when I visited there in 1959. I corresponded with her for a while and then I lost track of her.

Judith, having lived in Palestine, was accustomed to a great deal of social activity. During the somewhat idle days of the quarantine, she would round us up and lead us in dancing horas outside of the barracks to keep warm. We arrived in Birkenau in March and it was still quite cold. We would sing and dance and Judith was the one who kept us moving, and buoyed our spirits. She tried to help us to avoid depression and to keep us functioning.

Soon after arrival, we learned that for a ration of bread one could buy things. Prisoners who worked in storage barracks where the confiscated clothing was sorted would steal clothes. At the risk of their lives they would put on one or two new items underneath their clothes. If caught, they could be shot, depending on who caught them. In the evening, when their work day was finished and after their evening meal, they would enter our barracks to sell whatever they had. A lot depended upon what kind of transports[16] arrived. If a rich transport came in with a large quantity of good merchandise, it presented more of an incentive to steal.

The motto in camp was "Just don't get caught!" If you were, they could shoot you. Once you wore the stolen apparel, even though everyone knew where it came from, it was all right. For all their convoluted esthetic reasoning, the Nazis

16. Group of arrivals

couldn't abide our looking disheveled, dirty, and unkempt. This also provided them with a good reason to beat and kick us. The SS guards tended to do less hitting when they encountered prisoners who looked less disheveled, and dressed properly.

During this rather quiescent time in the quarantine period, twelve of us decided to pool our bread rations. Every day we divided eleven rations among the twelve of us, and used the twelfth ration to purchase an article of clothing in the evening. Thus we made sure that every twelve days each of us would acquire something decent to wear, without having to forego a full daily ration. We formed a buying committee and another one that supervised the distribution of the bread.

Once, during our quarantine period, someone sold us a dress. It was elegant, but out of place for our surroundings. The seller's asking price was two rations of bread. It was a great deal for us. We bargained and got the dress for one ration. We bought the dress because we felt that it could yield two items: the top could become a sweater, and the skirt could become a sleeveless vest. To do this we needed a crochet hook, which I crafted from a piece of wood which I shaved off the frame of our berth. To get the thread, I ripped part of the skirt. Lo and behold, we had the two pieces of apparel, and gave the top to the weakest girl in our group. She caught cold easily and sneezed all of the time. Someone else got the vest. Everyone was so impressed with our achievement that the following day the *Blockälteste* brought in three SS women guards to show them how creative we were. All of them overlooked the fact that this was stolen merchandise.

Three women prisoners shared the responsibility of running each of the barracks: the Blockälteste, who carried the major responsibility, her assistant (the *Verträterin*), and the secretary (the *Schreiberin*), who worked under her supervision.

The Blockälteste showcased us when she called all the SS women together to pridefully show them how I had made a crocheting needle out of a piece of wood cut from a board. If they had caught me cutting the board, they would have accused me of destroying property, and God knows what punishment they would have meted out to me, but they were positively in awe of my ingenuity.

As a result of this particular incident the Blockälteste became impressed with me, and I became the recipient of many of her favors. She overlooked some of my transgressions, such as my dealing with prisoners who were selling stolen merchandise. When it came to buying clothing or other items, the dealings resembled a stock market where a going price was established for particular items depending on what was available. She would advise me not to pay or trade too much of my bread because loads of materials came in on a given day and they would have to get rid of it for whatever they are able to get. She suggested that I *handel*[17] with them to get two things for one ration of bread.

By the time the two weeks had passed and we were ready to start working, all of us had wearable shoes and clothing that looked fairly respectable. We had a crochet needle with which we fixed things. For a few days, we felt like animals on display in a zoo; the SS guards would enter the barracks to see at firsthand how these odd looking prisoners behaved and what they did. They would comment among themselves about us as if we weren't present. We knew that it was important for us to look as presentable as possible.

17. Negotiate; bargain

Chapter 14

LIFE IN AUSCHWITZ-BIRKENAU

A DAY IN AUSCHWITZ started with being awakened at two a.m. to go to the latrine. At three a.m. various people were assigned from each section to kitchen duty, which included getting the so-called coffee. I had problems unless I could get a partner whose height was the same as mine. The containers were almost as tall as I was. They were very difficult to handle because the liquid was hot and if there was a disparity in our statures, there was spillage on my side.

The roads were not paved so whenever it rained, the mud reached up to our ankles. When we first arrived, they gave some of us Dutch shoes made of wood. It didn't take long to lose them in mud. Following the official start of spring on March twenty-first, our shoes were taken away because they said it would soon get warm. Unfortunately it was quite cold and we had to march barefoot.

At three a.m. those who were selected to pick up the coffee had to assemble in front of the barracks and go in a group to the kitchen. Some would hide or run away even though the Blockälteste would know who was assigned to this task. They would risk a beating for not joining the others, rather than hauling those heavy containers. When we got the coffee, we had those large bowls; the bigger they were, the more we got. If we got a full eight-inch bowl, we could drink a little and save the rest to wash ourselves. It didn't matter whether it was cold or hot, we would undress and wash. Your body had to be clean, because any spot on it was reason enough to send you to *Block*[18] 25.

After the "meal" we were all herded outside to line up for the counting: it was called *Zählappel*.[19] At about 4:30 a.m. we assembled in front of the barracks, five in a row, and remained in formation waiting for SS guards to count us. First the woman prisoner in charge of the barracks, the Blockälteste, her assistant, and her secretary would do the tallying, sometimes several times because some of the prisoners just decided to remain in the barracks upsetting the true count. Some

18. Block and barracks are used interchangeably. *Block* is the German word for barracks.
19. Roll call

prisoners were so depressed and spiritually demoralized that they would bury themselves in the straw mattresses to avoid attending the prisoner count.

When we were counted and a person was missing, we were all held responsible— it was a case of all for one. Those not present for the count knew this and were not trying to harm anyone, but when suddenly a cousin, mother, relative, or a *landsman*[20] in another barracks was found, one took her *schmatas*[21] and moved to the other barracks without telling anybody; because asking for permission would only lead to refusal. Since we all looked more or less alike and were almost anonymous, it took hours to locate the missing person. Until we found that prisoner, we were forced to stand outside, often for hours on end. It was terrible.

We once had a person missing and couldn't find her for a couple of hours. They took us all the way into the back of the camp to a small road that was paved with gravel. And we had to do exercises that lasted hours, though it felt like ages. We had to crawl on that rough surface to do push-ups and knee bends and all kinds of exercises. I remember how out of breath I was, how my knees hurt and bled from crawling on the gravel.

The basic rule was, one person's infraction subjects the whole group to severe penalties. Everyone was fearful of the retribution because sometimes it was extended over a period of many hours and was so severe that it was miraculous that there were any survivors.

If they noticed a victim struggling to survive, the beasts would sadistically increase the number and severity of the exercises until the unfortunate one dropped. When we saw a prisoner who was not walking fully erect, was straying off the line, or trespassing into forbidden territory, we would reprimand her, sometimes rather forcefully, just to prevent our collective punishment. Sometimes we spent hours looking for people who hid in corners, in ditches, in the latrines, and elsewhere. On a number of occasions, those who could no longer bear it rushed straight from the ditch to the electrified fence. The watchman, or the guard in his booth, either shot them or watched as they would kill themselves by touching the electrified fence. Time and again they counted us. The process lasted endless hours. You were forced to stand there at attention and if you weren't well, God help you. The SS man or SS woman entered to count and if you didn't stand erect, it was reason enough to beat or kick you. I was lucky. Early on I was able to stand.

Those of us who came from Cracow took care of each other. When someone took ill, unable to stand or march we lined up shoulder-to-shoulder, supporting the person who couldn't stand erect, even if only for the time it took for the count-

---

20. Countryman
21. Rags and miscellaneous items

ing. Two stronger girls would stand on either side of one who wasn't feeling well. We held each other up this way.

After the Zählappel, we were marched out to work. When I arrived, there was no orchestra. Later, when the second camp was opened, the Germans formed one. They drafted inmates with musical talent to entertain them on weekends, and to play marching music to speed the prisoners moving to and from work. There was only one such orchestra in Birkenau. We were required to march in rhythm. They would watch us intently and every misstep was looked upon as a serious infraction. It afforded a sadistic guard a reason to beat the unfortunate transgressor. If one's head was bowed, it was punched. Some learned, as I did, from the very beginning, that you could avoid an assault if you walked straight, kept clean, and looked the tormentors straight in the eye.

We worked on projects that made no sense at all. We carried bricks and sand for miles from one place to another. In the fall and in the spring the prisoners would each receive some sort of a coat. At work we wore it back to front. The front would form an apron and one prisoner would load it full of sand until the coat and the sand pulled us all the way down. Then they wanted us to walk straight, and we would march for hours, dumping our overload only to have the pile moved to a different place. I think this is what I saw when I originally arrived in the camp—people walking in long rows, weary, plodding and weighted down. That took a great deal out of us.

By lunchtime we were exhausted and hungry. The bread ration that was supposed to last a whole day, was completely devoured by some as soon as it was received. Those who had more control saved some bread for later.

During our working hours we were not allowed to attend to our personal needs. This was another of the horrendous physiological problems with which we had to cope. We were permitted to go to the latrine only in the morning when we woke, at lunch when we had a break, and in the evening when we returned to camp, only three times a day. When we walked barefoot in the cold, and there was still snow and frost in April, our feet became painfully cold, and it was impossible to control the bladder.

The first time I walked out to work, I needed to relieve myself and there was no way I could do so because we were still marching. I knew that if I soiled my pants, I would be beaten. If I asked permission, I'd also be hit. No matter what I did, it was wrong. I had to go, and said to the girl next to me that I would burst if I didn't. She warned me not to do so but hold on until we reached our destination. Sometimes when we got to work, it was possible to hide in the bushes. I could no longer bear it so I went over to one of the German guards and told him of my predicament. He started to laugh and said: "So, make in the pants." I said: "If I do so, you'll beat me." He replied, "Well, if you run away, I'll beat you too." I don't know how, but talking things out had become one of my special skills, and after I finished reasoning with him, he let me fall back from the group and hide behind a bush. No one believed that he'd permit me to do this. For many years after liberation, I had a problem with having to wait to use the bathroom.

Another lesson that I learned in conjunction with those restrictions was the fact that people couldn't really survive alone. In addition to luck, constitutional strength, and emotional stability, it was important to have a friend, somebody to cover for you, somebody to literally lean on. For instance, even with asking an SS man to let me go off into the bushes, I counted on my friend to intercede in my behalf.

When we broke for lunch—whatever food we got, we finished in a minute. The food was brought to us in cannisters containing whatever kind of unsavory soup they cooked that day. We had about a half hour for lunch.

Sometimes some overseers were quite friendly. Every once in a while they would chat with some of the prisoners. Many Germans liked music and singing, and they would ask us to sing marching songs when we were outside the camp gates marching to work. Sometimes when we sat around after lunch they would ask us if we knew German or Polish songs or any other ones. They enjoyed our singing for them. Sometimes we would do so just to ease the tension. The same person wouldn't always accompany us on the work details, but whenever one did, he would remember that in this particular group there was someone who used to sing a song that he liked. Some of the German overseers lived near the camp grounds. Those were usually *Volksdeutschen,* Poles of German descent who knew some Polish songs, and they would request them. Paradoxically, they would beat us when our backs were not straight while carrying bricks or they would find some reason to torment us when we worked. Then when we would sit down for lunch, they would ask us if we could sing this or that song. After lunch we worked for another couple of hours before we returned to camp for the evening counting.

Each group that walked out was called a *Kommando* unit, and there were several hundred people in a unit. As we walked out of the camp, each German guard who led us reported to the front office: "I am taking out five hundred prisoners." Then, when we returned, they were responsible for bringing back exactly the same number. God pity them if they brought back less. There were rare instances when some tried to escape. Then we could stand through an entire night waiting for the return of the missing one. They would either hunt down the escapee or inform us that they did so. The waiting seemed endless. In any event, when we returned, the front office was notified by the guard that he was bringing back the same number of prisoners that he took out. We were counted. And then we returned to our barracks.

At six p.m. we were counted again. The procedure of the morning was repeated in the evening. We lined up in rows of five in front of the barracks, and the secretary counted us. If the number was correct, she reported this to the main office (eventually I became a Schreiberin and that is how I became well acquainted with the entire procedure).

After that we had our dinner, followed by about an hour during which we were free to do what we wanted. People would go from one Block to another, visiting relatives or friends, or buying and selling merchandise from, and/or to the people who worked in the area where clothing was selected and sorted. This was a very important part of the day. My friend Judith and I would ask the Blockälteste for a patrol assignment. This job permitted us to walk around just in front of our barracks or on the main street for an hour or so after curfew.

The first time we went on patrol it was a beautiful, starry night. The lighting around the camp area was bright. We talked, always on the same subject. Does anyone know where we are? Is there anybody who cares? How is it possible that so many people can exist in one area undetected? Doesn't the neighboring village know that we are here? The existence of so many people can't be a secret. We wondered about this and about the trains arriving constantly. If only someone would let America know what was going on, perhaps they would come and bomb the camps. We walked and talked: she wondered what her husband was doing and I wondered about my father in America, who was free. Sometimes we would joke, and she would say: "Well, your father probably just had dinner and went out to see a good movie, or to a party." Our walk would last about an hour. Sometimes, when we didn't get the patrol assignment, we went out and pretended we had it, because we needed to get out of that claustrophobia-inducing setting.

I remember an incident during what was called a *Blocksperre,* which was a curfew confining everyone to their barracks after a certain hour. It was summertime, and newcomers had just been assigned to our barracks. Two of the newly arrived women decided to take a walk. I approached them like an all-knowing veteran—I had been in camp for six months or so.

I spoke to them in Polish: "Do you know that we are not allowed to be out of doors?"

One of them was tall; she looked down at me and said, "Who are you to tell me what to do?"

That evening I had been given the responsibility for the Block by the Blockälteste who requested that I get these two women back to where they belong. It turned out that they were either two cousins or two close friends from two differ-ent barracks and they had made an appointment to meet each other at this time to talk for a few minutes before going to bed.

They began to berate me, calling me rather nasty names and asking who ap-pointed me boss. I remonstrated: "Would you please get inside before all of us are punished."

Being new, they weren't aware of the consequences that might follow. One said something quite derogatory. I don't remember exactly what it was, but it did stir the suppressed anger in me. I had been given the authority to tell them to go in-doors and here they were refusing to do so. I aimed a blow at one of them. I had to jump up to hit her. Her nose started to bleed. I was very upset, even more so than the one who was hurt. Until the end of my camp internment I felt awful for having done that. One of them I believe was German, and German Jews had such utter contempt for Polish Jews that they refused to take directions from us.

This incident taught me a lesson that I never forgot. I never again tried to hit anybody. I never thought that I had that much power, but she was either a bleeder or I really didn't know my own strength.

Chapter 15

MORE ABOUT LIFE IN AUSCHWITZ-BIRKENAU

WHENEVER I THINK ABOUT Birkenau, I remember how painful was our daily existence, how enervated we became with the Zählappelen and the working conditions. The effort to stay alive was strenuous beyond belief. But in order to function, I somehow have to bury these memories of a day that seemed to have no end. It had no beginning either, because we slept and had nightmares and we were afraid. And when we awakened the fears were still with us. We lived like shadows.

One day the guards decided to organize an orchestra and proceeded to look for people who could play musical instruments among the newly arrived transports. They had no great difficulty in finding talented musicians. It was a deeply upsetting experience and yet at times it could also be an uplifting one. Officially, we weren't allowed to listen to the orchestra, except when they played marching music as we left for and returned from work. They concertized every Sunday afternoon in front of the officers' quarters where we were forbidden to be, but we managed to sneak up to listen to the music whenever we could, if we didn't have work.

On Sundays, when we didn't have to work, we would usually take care of our clothing, washing and sewing, or just doing nothing. Sometimes we were permitted to go for a walk but not near the orchestra. Under the pretext of having to get from one place to another, we would walk over to listen. The experience was more important for the older prisoners than for the newer arrivals. They were too overwhelmed to long for music. Those of us who had seniority desired some reminder of a past that we all thought would never return. But we hoped, and I quietly prayed for miracles and for survival.

During free time, when I was a regular laborer, we liked to get together in the upper berths with those of our friends who had been there for a long time. There was no one above us, just the roof, so there was room to stand up. During these gatherings we would fantasize about a future that might never be. Sometimes we sang Jewish or Polish folk songs or even pop tunes. Most of the time however, we tried to support and encourage the weak and those ready to give up fighting.

Food and what we would eat if and when we regained our freedom was a favorite subject.

Some prisoners just couldn't take the uncertainty of not knowing what might happen next; many of them broke down mentally. Once hope was gone, some found it impossible to cope.

While in camp I was sick twice. A month or two after my arrival I awoke with a fever and a sore throat. I said to my friend that I didn't know how I was going to be able to get to work. I knew that I could not remain in the barracks because those who did, and were caught, were sent to Block 25. If one were lucky, the Blockälteste or a German guard in a good mood might transfer a prisoner to the so-called hospital instead of Block 25. My friend told me not to worry and that another friend who was in our berth would help her to get me out. Sometimes, once you reached your work place, it was possible to bribe an SS guard to allow a sick person to lie down on the side where one could not be seen.

What we worried about was how I was going to be able to march out to work without breaking the rhythm of my group. With my high temperature, I could hardly stand, let alone march. But I managed through the count in front of the exit gate because two other girls walked shoulder-to-shoulder with me to keep me upright and moving. The strength that one can muster in a life-threatening situation is unbelievable. As we marched, I felt the pressure of their arms on mine. They kept counting rhythmically in Polish, "One-two, one-two, left-right, left-right, make it." "Just through the gate," they kept whispering, "just through the gate. Just another couple of steps," and I kept muttering through my clenched teeth, "I can't make it." I couldn't lean on them because that would indicate that I could not walk. Eventually, I did make it.

Another incident involved a crazy SS man outside of the camp. We were working in a small group. And he insisted on having some sort of stupid entertainment. This happened during the entire week when I wasn't feeling well. He decided that he wanted to see whether we could jump over a ditch that surrounded the fields in which we worked. He announced that those who couldn't make it over the ditch, would go directly to Barracks 25. He lined us up in a row, one behind another. I can't remember now if he actually took anyone to the dreaded Barracks 25. All I recall is thinking that if I didn't get to the other side of that ditch, it would be the end of my life. I managed to jump, my fever notwithstanding. I often wondered how anyone could devise so many unbearable ways of mistreating and punishing prisoners.

When someone was missing during roll call, the Germans would send hounds after the absentee. Very few prisoners escaped.

I was rather resourceful, I think, but perhaps not in the sense of accomplishing heroic deeds. I tried to obey whatever I was ordered to do in the best way I could. Thus I avoided being hit, kicked, or mistreated by those who supervised us. Singing helped; a good sense of humor was also effective.

After a Kommando of one hundred walked out to do a job, the result upon completion was that at least twenty would become physically unfit for anything. The sick were sometimes transferred to the so-called hospital, sometimes to Block 25. It was so easy to succumb. The atmosphere was conducive to breaking one's body and one's spirit.

If it weren't for close friends, such as the girls who actually carried me out and kept me erect on the march, I couldn't have made it. It wasn't enough to look after yourself; two eyes were not enough to see every danger. Sometimes when we were digging ditches, for instance, we would try not to attract the attention of the guards because whenever they saw two people who were too close, they would try to separate them. But we watched out for each other. A message would come through quietly, "This one is watching, this one—look at his eyes, he is sitting and probably thinking of doing something crazy, so watch out, don't step out of line."

It was just terrible how those in command would think of torturous ways of ordering us to perform unnecessary tasks because very few things that we accomplished in camp were really constructive or meaningful, except perhaps for the sorting of clothing. At least there was a system in the operation. I never worked at this job, but I was told that some of those that did would not only steal, but also try to ruin some of the items selected to be sent to Germany, just to render them useless.

When I now read the papers and find statements by so-called researchers who insist that the camps existed only in our imaginations, I become livid with rage. How could anyone deny the existence of the Holocaust? It is beyond my comprehension. I envy that great, great spokesman for all survivors, Elie Wiesel, who chronicles our story in such poetic and moving prose. I wish I could do a better job of recording my experiences.

Chapter 16

AUSCHWITZ:
SPECIAL JOBS

THERE WERE SEVERAL special jobs for which only a few prisoners were needed. The SS men would select twenty, thirty, or forty people to clean the offices or work in small gardens or individual homes. Other jobs were more strenuous, but we did not complain when we were assigned to construction work. At least it was the kind of job that made sense. Once we were ordered to demolish a house, for which we used a heavy boom. As difficult as this was, there was a purpose to what we were doing. When we were finished, we felt that we had accomplished something useful. It was undoubtedly better than carrying sand back and forth.

Once we were assigned to work in a swamp. We had no idea as to what we were going to do. When we reached the site, we found that we had to enter the murky swamp. It was slimy and horrendous, and there were leeches in the brackish water. We screamed because, once you went in, the guards would beat you if you tried to get out. The Germans were having a hilarious time watching us. They said, "Look at those Jews; they are scared of the water." Even now, I can recall the pain and fear that overcame us. But we had no choice. We were forced to dive in and do whatever they wanted. It was terrible, and every day there was something else of an equally horrifying nature.

Sometimes, some of the prisoners who were not chosen for work remained in camp. This posed some risk, because occasionally the guards who had no specific assignment on that day decided to inspect the camp and check why there were prisoners who were not "gainfully employed." To them, those who were not at work were automatically useless. They called them *Muselman*, which meant useless and decrepit. Such a spontaneous inspection led to minor selections during which the SS guards would send many of the nonworking prisoners to Barracks 25 to await transfer to the gas chambers at a later date.

Sometimes, when we returned from work, we heard that Dr. Mengele was expected for an inspection of the camp. That meant that a major selection *(Selekcja)* was planned. When he made the selections, we were assembled outside of our barracks. For him and other occasional bigwigs involved in the selection, we were ordered to disrobe, no matter what the weather. He would always carry a whip and the distance between him and the prisoners would be the length of that whip. He would use the whip to pick up the breast to see whether there were any infectious spots underneath. Any little mark on the body was considered a symptom of typhus,[22] an illness of which the German soldiers were deeply afraid. It could be one or two spots. Usually those were not really typhus marks, but it did not matter. Some said that they were bites, but no one paid any attention to what the prisoner said. That was another thing I learned early on . . . not to scratch no matter how badly it itched. Any break in the skin could mean the gas chamber.

That was the most horrendous thing . . . this meticulous inspection of the entire body, the search for the spot with a flip of the whip, following which they would order the unfortunate one to the collection Barracks 25. This of course meant separations from relatives and friends. When the examiner said, "to the left," or "to the right," there was no appeal. Each time a selection took place, and it happened quite frequently, part of the humanity in each of us died. We learned to maintain our cleanliness. As long as one had a *schmata* to use as a washcloth, one could avoid exuding an offensive odor. It was difficult for some who needed more food and could not spare any of their morning drink for washing. Sometimes it wasn't only Dr. Mengele who visited; there were other SS VIPs who showed up. At times, when they arrived to count us during the Zählappel and noticed someone who didn't look well, or who was not standing erect, the prisoner would be pulled out even if no official selection was taking place.

We could buy certain luxury items that we didn't need for ourselves, but which we could use as a bribe for the overseer who would look the other way while one rested, or went into the bushes. Occasionally, some of us did negotiate with a few of the guards. There were some prisoners who conducted a mutually profitable business with the SS men. They would request that a prisoner with access to something they wanted steal it for them. Some of the prisoners were able to earn a great deal of extra food working with the guards.

Sometimes after dealing with someone who allowed certain liberties for favors rendered, one was suddenly transferred to another job. Inside jobs such as cleaning, sweeping, or office work were plum assignments. Once a prisoner failed to supply her guard with what he requested, he arranged a change of job for her. That was another lesson we learned in camp—there were no secrets there. If you

---

22. Typhus is a highly contagious, flea-borne disease that appears in prisons and in army units where personal hygiene is poor. The earliest symptoms are spots or a rash. Often called "prison fever," it is greatly feared because the mortality rate can be high, particularly among those who are already debilitated.

had one, you had better keep it to yourself, because anybody else who might know could use it against you.

I am good with languages, I learn very quickly. I became proficient in conversing in Czech and this served me well because most of the prisoners in charge of the barracks were of Czechoslovakian descent; they were among the first brought to the camp. Many of them perished, but the staunchest of them who survived were eventually assigned by the Germans to run the camp.

The seniority system resembled the one used by the army. The longer you were there, the better the likelihood that you would get a better position. Thus most of the Czechoslovakian girls were put in charge of barracks or work groups, because they arrived in Birkenau with the first transports. I had no problem in communicating with them. I tried to be helpful. I did what I was told. When I was ordered to bring the coffee, or the dinner, or anything else, I obeyed. I didn't hide. After a while the Czechs in charge realized that I was reliable. When there was something important to do, they would come to me and I would try to help them. Many who came from small towns or villages were very young girls without much schooling. At times they would ask me to help them arrange lists of prisoners in numerical order.

A beautiful Czechoslovakian girl was in charge of the *Lager*.[23] The Germans worked very closely with her. Any instructions or orders that emanated from the main office reached this particular girl. Her title was *Lagerälteste*, or senior prisoner in charge of the camp. Once, while I was helping our secretary I overheard them talking about a position that might be available soon—an office was being opened and a bookkeeper would be needed. I didn't know much about keeping books, but I did have a general idea. My family once owned a business that employed a bookkeeper.

One day the Blockälteste approached me and asked, "Would you be interested in applying for a bookkeeping job? You'll have to take a test. Would you be willing to take the exam?"

I said, "What do I have to lose . . . I will take it."

Some time elapsed until the plan was crystallized; then the list of candidates was submitted. The Blockälteste, I suppose, had recommended me. I was called. There were perhaps twenty other girls who applied.

The examination was divided into two parts: a written one and an oral one. We were brought into the main office for the test. It was administered on a one-on-one basis. An SS man sat behind a desk with his revolver handy. I received a warn-

---

23. Camp

ing. If I was lying about being a bookkeeper, he was eminently qualified to detect a falsehood, and God help me if I did so, because his revolver was loaded. The minute he caught me in a lie, he threatened to use the pistol. I was terribly frightened. I didn't know what to expect. I wasn't really a bookkeeper, I had only a cursory knowledge garnered from hearing my parents discussing it in relation to our business. But I really had no choice, so I opted to risk it.

The SS examiner was a tall, good-looking man with icy blue eyes. He looked straight into mine. The revolver he placed on his desk contributed to my unease. However, I pretended to be self-assured. He reminded me repeatedly that if he caught me lying, I would be shot immediately. He produced a piece of paper. My heart stopped and my knees felt rubbery, anticipating the questions that were going to be asked. They turned out to be problems in simple arithmetic. I suppose he didn't know much about bookkeeping either. The first task dealt with figuring cubic feet. The second part consisted of a rather simple mathematical proposition about two trains traveling in opposite directions at different speeds, and I was supposed to figure out when the trains would meet. I don't know how long I sat there, but I realized that I had better be careful with my multiplication. In camp one's demeanor was very important. I was petrified but I pretended to be calm and collected. He sat there and watched me, then he rose and marched around the room, observing me from behind to see what I was doing. I finished, handed him my paper and walked out.

Other women were waiting outside. Of course, we were not allowed to talk to each other, but the women saw that I was still alive and took strength and encouragement from that fact. When the test was over we were told that we had to take an oral examination in addition. It didn't take place immediately. The waiting was difficult and anxiety-producing. But there was an ancillary benefit from the delay. While we waited for the oral examination, we were not allowed to work outside of the camp. We were confined inside the barracks and told to wait until we were called. That didn't mean that we were idle. Every few hours a German would have some chore for us, enter the barracks and ask the Blockälteste for the number of prisoners required for the task. We were called *verfügbar*, which means "for disposition"; that is, we were prisoners held for a special assignment.

While waiting in the barracks, I befriended the Blockälteste, her assistant, and her secretary. They decided to use me to help them cut the bread. As in any business, if you delegate work, you do less yourself. The bread would arrive in full one-pound loaves, which had to be cut into four quarters for distribution to the prisoners on their return from work. They would slice the bread in a special way; one thin slice was cut out from the center. The thin slice was appropriated by the people in charge of the barracks, making it possible for them to use their regular ration for barter. The remainder of the bread was cut into quarters and distributed to the prisoners.

Sometimes the bread was difficult to cut, depending upon how much ersatz was put into it. When it seemed as though the bread would crumble, we made sure to cut it in the presence of the prisoners so that they might see that we personally were not cheating them. It was horrible to get only a few pitiable crumbs.

Eventually, the day for the oral examination was announced and once again the anxiety was almost unbearable, but there was no choice.

When we reached the main office, a tall SS man, neatly attired, carrying a whip and a holstered gun, assembled us in front of the office. This time they did not lead us in. He arranged us in a row according to height. I was literally the last one on the line and he, brandishing his whip, posed a question to the first one, who was the tallest. Depending upon his mood, or how she answered, he would kick or whip her if he felt her answer or posture wasn't correct. Some of the applicants were older than I, and I didn't know if there was anyone else who had lied about being a bookkeeper. I was lucky to be near the end of the line.

If the prisoner did not know the answer, he would call out, "Next, next, next." This gave the next person time to think. The one before me was asked a question, the answer to which she did not know. I didn't know whether he would ask me the same question or not; he just stood there thinking. Then he hit her lightly over her legs with his whip and cursed her. The Germans apparently loved delivering speeches. He spoke about her apparent false claim to being a bookkeeper and her failure to know the answer to such a basic question. I supposed that it was simple enough; he wanted to know what types of bookkeeping there were. His yelling at my predecessor gave me time to review what little I knew of the subject. Then he asked me the same question to which I fortunately knew the answer. Once you answered the question correctly you were taken out of the line; that was it. I passed the examination, and I was put back into the barracks where I continued to be *verfügbar*. We waited. When guards arrived with requests for people to work, it was forbidden to take me out of camp because I had passed the examination and was waiting to be called for my new job any day. I could only be taken somewhere locally so that I could be reached in a hurry. This situation lasted for at least a couple of weeks.

While I was waiting for this job to materialize, someone came back from working outside of the camp and reported that the Germans were building a new factory in which they planned to produce artificial rubber and that product would be made from a certain plant. Something like *Coxagus*. It looked like a dandelion, the common little yellow weed. When the stem was broken it contained a milky liquid, which, when mixed with other chemicals, would provide the formula for the artificial rubber. We were told that in conjunction with this plan there would be openings in this new laboratory. They would need experts in the fields of biology and zoology. I was certainly not well versed in either of these sciences but I had had an excellent biology/zoology teacher when I attended grammar school. She taught students to pay attention to details and she instilled in us many worthwhile ideas. We hated her, but she was a very fine teacher, and taught not from books alone. She would take us out into the fields to show us how much more effective was this method of study.

The Blockälteste informed me that an exam was scheduled and advised me to take it. I had passed one test. I was already an "educated" prisoner, and the worst that could happen to me was that I wouldn't get the job. I hadn't yet been selected for the bookkeeping job. And rumors were that it no longer existed. So I decided that I would pretend that I have a doctorate in zoology. After the first test, rumors spread that one really didn't have to be so expert. This time many more people applied for the exam in zoology. The number of those deemed eligible was cut. And perhaps because I was friendly with the Czechoslovakian girls, I remained among those awaiting the examination.

One day I was taken to that new laboratory. I reasoned that the Germans were not going to employ the Jewish prisoners for important work. I further thought that they required people to clean the laboratory and the instruments. I noticed all sorts of microscopes, vials, and little glass items. I knew that these were fragile and had to be handled with great care. I realized that it probably was for this that they wanted us.

When I came into the lab, I saw a young Polish woman. This scared me a little. When you place one prisoner in charge of another, the one with higher rank gets power-hungry and very cocky. She turned out to be a very nice, soft-spoken woman who had a self-assured mien. We all waited outside while she called us in individually. I walked in and noticed a plant on her desk. She asked me to tell her everything I knew about the plant. I do not know where my knowledge came from. It must have been buried way in the deep recesses of my brain where it lay dormant for years. I answered her questions correctly. I wasn't quite sure but I spoke about a plant that I did know: its family, the type of its leaf. Then I said: "I think it looks very much like that, so it might be part of the same family." She said: "Yes, you are right . . . you couldn't give me the correct name but you came close enough . . . fine." I had passed that exam also. I was double *verfügbar* when I left. There were many who did not pass. I think what saved me was the fact that I spoke about something I really knew. She told me it would take some time before the laboratory was finished. It was a new building and the odor of fresh cut wood permeated the entire area.

After the test we were sent back to the barracks and again, we waited and waited. As it turned out, neither the bookkeeping nor the zoology job materialized. I became more active in helping the girls in charge, assisting them in organizing all the activities and compiling various lists. The secretary wasn't very sure of her math. She really welcomed my help and her appreciation was quite evident. I received a little more bread, and I got greater consideration. I felt privileged and appreciated the good treatment, but I didn't take advantage. Even if I had no assignment, I would ask for something to do because I never knew who might come in and catch me idling. If I did lie down, it would be in the Blockälteste's room,[24] not in the barracks, so that I could be warned if a guard dropped in. When the Germans arrived, they would zoom right into the barracks to look for any infraction of the rules. You were assumed to be guilty before they could even prove anything.

We heard rumors that they were going to enlarge the camp and open up another one for women. We were in Lager A and they were opening Lager B. The Blockälteste came to me one day and said that she had spoken to the Lagerälteste who confirmed that the B Lager would be opened soon. Similar to camp A, there would be twenty-five barracks in the new camp. The remaining Czechoslovakian girls who had not been assigned to an inside job would probably get the available positions of Blockälteste, their assistants, and secretaries. Now, one of the girls who was assistant to the Blockälteste of my barracks got an assignment as Blockälteste in camp B, and went to the Lagerälteste to request that I become her secretary. She had observed me at work and knew that I was responsible. Her request was granted and thus ended my hard physical labor in the camp. Until the end of my incarceration at Auschwitz, I was a secretary. I was good at that job, and they knew it.

Sometimes it was a most difficult chore to get all the numbers entered correctly on one list. I remember one particular day when a transport arrived from a small Polish town. A messenger from the front office notified my Blockälteste that some of the prisoners would be admitted into our barracks. She was therefore advised to go to the processing center and pick up a given number of prisoners. As the barracks secretary, I accompanied her. We waited at the exit door of the sauna for our contingent. Unfortunately the simple task of receiving the new prisoners assigned to us turned out to be a major undertaking, as the new people were di-

---

24. At the entrance to each of the barracks were two small rooms, one for the staff, and the other (Kammerstube or pantry) for storage of bread, clothing, etc.

vided into several groups to be sent to several barracks quite arbitrarily. Many families were separated and people were running from one barracks to another seeking to stay with their own family. We knew that on the allotment sheet we had several prisoners transferred to us from other barracks, a couple of hundred new assignments, and some from our own barracks transferred to the hospital. In the evening we started to collate our population chart and to count the number of people we should have, and how many were actually with us; we didn't resolve our problem until the early hours of the morning. We had to walk from berth to berth in the night with a small flashlight to count the people who were asleep to ascertain how many people we really had. That was difficult too because some people left their berth to go to the latrine. We finally concluded that the number they listed for us on the paper, and those we counted in their various sleeping areas, tallied.

The assistant Blockälteste and I tried to get the final list down on paper. It was long past midnight. Since we were forbidden to have any lights on at night, we covered the window with an army blanket. There must have been a small hole in the blanket which we did not detect. An SS guard on patrol noticed our light. The assistant Blockälteste and I were working and smoking, which was strictly forbidden. We would use bobby pins to hold the cigarette so we could avoid staining our fingertips with nicotine. That night we were far too busy to use the bobby pins. We worked in a small room that served as a pantry. We sat at the table, which we used to cut the bread, smoking fiendishly, she at one end and I at the other. We were nervous and tired. Suddenly, the door flew open and the most sadistic SS man, *Raportführer* Taube, entered. The assistant Blockälteste almost reflexively put the cigarette behind her back. I did nothing because I was sitting with my back to the door, and did not see him enter. So she hid her cigarette and I remained seated there like a *schlemazel*[25] holding the cigarette in my hand. He stepped towards me with his whip raised and said, "What the hell is the matter with you, *du Verfluchte Jude?*" How dare I blow smoke straight into his face when I knew that he could shoot me, beat me, and consign me to Barracks 25? How dare I be so arrogant? I had to think quickly so I said, "Look, you walked in and you saw me with that cigarette. Wouldn't it be stupid if I tried to hide it, after you spotted me . . . I give you more credit for intelligence." He stood there rather surprised because very few people talked back to him. He looked at me and said, "You know what, you've got a point." He called me *"Schreiberin mit eine fresche Schnauze."*[26]

---

25. A poor unfortunate loser
26. With a fresh mouth

Starting that night, he and I developed a certain rapport. Not that he was any nicer to me; he could curse me whenever he felt like it, but he never hit me from that time on. When one walked on the main street, one never knew whether to pass him on the right side or on the left. Depending on his mood, if one passed him on the wrong side, he could knock you to the ground and beat you. When he met me after that night, and I happened to be in the wrong place, he pretended not to see me.

That night, however, when he entered and realized that it was already one o'clock in the morning, he asked what we were doing. We told him, because there was no point in lying. He acknowledged that it was very complicated. He added that if it weren't for the damn Jewish newcomers running here and there, we wouldn't have any problems. From then on, when he was on duty at night, he would make it a point to check out our barracks. We didn't always have to work that late but we tried to prepare our tally in the evening because I had to deliver it to the main office at about three a.m.

When there were two of us and only himself, and it was the middle of the night and he felt no pressure, he liked to sit inside and talk, especially in the fall and winter when it was very cold outside. He once told us as we sat there working on the tally that nobody was going to come out of that camp alive.

He said, "Don't be stupid, we are not going to lose the war."

Sometimes we would say to him, "Let's make believe."

He would answer, "You know, if you mentioned 'make believe' to somebody else, you would not see the sunrise tomorrow morning." He reminded us that some of the work that we had done included laying mines in the camp in the main and side streets. "When we are convinced the Germans will lose the war, we will blow up this place."

I said, "What about you?"

He said, "Well, we will find some way of getting out and if we can't, we'll go with you; in any event we are not going to let you survive." He pointed to our identifying tattoos and said, "Especially all of you with low numbers who have been in this camp for a long period of time, you must be destroyed because YOU will be the witnesses."

There were heartaches attendant upon being in charge. No one listened; people were sick. There were those you cared for and you wanted to help. However, it was not always possible. For instance, once during the processing of a new transport from a Polish town, I noticed three girls who came to our barracks. They looked and behaved a bit differently from the rest. One was an extremely beautiful girl. At the time they arrived, the rule of shaving the complete head was changed to cutting the hair very short. The three girls, Tania, Lusia, and Genia, were sisters. One of them was already bereft of all her hair because she questioned or answered someone in the wrong way; for that she was shaved as punishment. They would stand aside and patiently await their turn. Other prisoners were so combative; as the bread rations or clothing were being distributed, they would forcefully claim their share. They would almost tear off the hands that were serving.

When these girls were told to stand in line for dresses or trousers, they waited, while the others rushed to the pile of clothing and pulled haphazardly. Many behaved like vultures, acting indiscriminately in the name of self-preservation. The philosophy that prevailed was that if you didn't take care of yourself, nobody else would. Those three girls stood there transfixed not knowing what hit them. Of course, they were quite upset because they were separated from their parents, realizing that they would probably never see their loved ones again. I liked them. Before we brought out the clothing from storage, or from a delousing, I would sort through the apparel and select the better items for them. I gave these young women preferential treatment.

The youngest girl got into trouble once during a selection, because she was not too well developed and looked very young, which she was. So they separated the three sisters. The youngest was put to the side for transfer to Barracks 25 to await her death in the gas chamber. This happened some time after they arrived in camp. The two older sisters came to me and cried bitterly. I didn't know what to do, but I promised to try to help. Fortunately, the overseer, Taube, was patrolling those who were slated for Block 25. I considered that a good omen. He also knew that I was a Schreiberin; I decided to use this as an excuse for approaching him with the master list in hand so that it looked very official.

I covered my mouth with the document so that no one would notice that I was pleading with him. I told him that one girl being held inside was a relative of mine. I acknowledged that sometimes he could not help either (I tried to portray him as the good one) but if it was at all possible for him to get her out of that group, I would really appreciate it very much. It meant, of course, that I would have to get something for him.

Then he started to yell, pretending that I had offended him in some way. Picking up the whip he said, "What do you want? You are not supposed to be here. Those are the people who should, and don't ask me any questions. Try the other guard." His screaming confused and scared everyone. While issuing his orders he maneuvered her out of the dreaded group slated for Block 25 back into the group with her sisters.

I was eventually separated from the three sisters. They moved on to a better job in *Kanada,* a storage place where the new possessions that people brought with them were sorted and stored. For awhile we were able to keep track of one another, but I was inside and they were working; and at the end of the day there were prisoner's chores to be done.

At another time there was the mother of a girl with whom I went to school who was also ordered to Block 25 and whom I was able to rescue from the condemned Block. Again, we were lucky that Taube was present. He was terrible and feared by all. People ran when they saw him coming. If they could dig a hole in which to hide, they would gladly do so. However, I knew how to deal with him without making him angry and, when necessary, making him act a little more humane. I told him she was my aunt, and, by causing a commotion, he was able to maneuver her out.

One day, as I was processing a newly arrived transport, I recognized Mira who went to school with me. She was doomed, and on her way to the gas chamber. Mira had beautiful green eyes; she was tall, slim, and intelligent. She was a loving friend too and when I saw her go I was disconsolate. I ran and marched alongside her. I tried to release her from the group, but the supervisor, whom I didn't know, screamed at me. I couldn't tell him that I wanted her out. Instead, I said that I saw somebody I knew, and could I please talk to her. She was in the middle of the row but they allowed her to move to the end so I could walk next to her. I tried, but I couldn't save her. The reason I was given was that she had already been designated to go to the gas chamber, that he needed to account for a prescribed number of people and he just couldn't let anyone out. He said, "Unless you want to exchange her for somebody else." Whom could I pick? We cried—both of us. She saw that I was trying. A great deal of screaming was directed at me but at least I had an opportunity to speak with her. She was a beautiful girl; an only child. Her father was an older gentleman. They were not poor. He had been married previously, had grown children, and then wed her mother. She had already lived in a ghetto, or some other camp. She also had Aryan features and had apparently spent some time on the outside of the ghetto. I deeply lamented the fact that I couldn't rescue her.

Chapter 17

BLOCK 25

I FIND IT EXTREMELY distressing that my attempt to record what happened to me in Auschwitz is so difficult and that I have such a problem in recalling my painful experiences. They remain with me, and when I try to remember, I have to concentrate deeply to jog my memory. Emotionally I can feel the tremendous pain that was inflicted upon me. However, when I record the events, the task seems almost insurmountable. If I had to live with these anguished memories daily, it would be impossible to function normally or adequately.

I recently received a letter from a friend in Israel with whom I had not corresponded for a long time. She reminded me of something that happened in Auschwitz. She asked if I still sang that sad song about Hawaii, and I recalled that sometimes when we were out working in the fields, we sang songs to buoy our spirits. The Germans would request the melodies they liked, and if we did not know them, they taught them to us. This particular song I learned from one of the guards during our lunch break; it was about a man longing to be on the sunny beaches of Hawaii. I used to do the singing, and I did so quite often. It was woefully nostalgic. There were songs that I learned in school, some of them in German and Polish. I believe that these songs sustained me. They conjured up images that were nonexistent in Auschwitz. It was such a barren place. There was no life there, no grass, no trees, no birds, just dark gray skies. Even on sunny days, the sky was darkened by the smoke billowing out of the five chimneys continually.

Outside of the camp proper, there was a patch of forest where they processed those condemned to the gas chambers. The trees were probably situated there to block the view from the outside. It looked a little greener. Our camp Birkenau or *Brzezinki* got its name from these birch trees. I was there only once because I had heard that a transport from Lublin was arriving, and my mother had relatives in that city. I knew that going there would not change anything, because once someone was transferred to that part of the camp, her fate was already sealed; I had never heard about anyone that was taken out of there. At that time, I had already succeeded in pulling two people from a line who were slated for Block 25, the holding station for those condemned to the gas chamber. I felt that it was worth another try. We were told to tell the newcomers that they were being registered for camp. Knowing that this was not true and that they were destined for the showers from which they would never return was quite difficult to endure.

I would usually avoid these assignments using my designation as a Schreiberin as an excuse. I asked to go because I thought perhaps this time I would find somebody from my hometown or some of my own people. There were masses of people and it was most difficult to find anyone. I hoped that even if I failed to see them, they might see me. Some of us went to talk with the new arrivals. They asked many questions pertaining to camp life and other matters. It really didn't matter if we told them that life in the camp was horrible. They would not have believed us in any event, because the registrars were, like me, people who had been working for the last several months inside the camp; we didn't look emaciated or dirty.

As we sat and talked with a group of people, one newcomer was wearing (I don't know how she passed through all those Germans with it) a thin gold chain and on it was a little enamel charm. It depicted the two tablets containing the ten commandments. It was colorful and inspirational. I noticed it, and a woman who accompanied me asked the girl whether she could see it and then if she could have it. The girl refused because it was a gift from her grandmother. At that point the woman became quite angry. It was tragic watching the struggle. The girl who was fated for the gas chamber wasn't really aware of that fact.

The camp woman became so irate that she blurted out in anger, "You will not be using it anyhow. Someone else is going to take it away from you."

We understood her innuendo, but I doubt if the girl who owned the chain did. Another woman and I walked her away from there because it was terrible. The prisoner who wanted the chain would probably not be able to wear it, because if a German saw her wearing it he would take it away. It was, however, an irrational desire on her part to have that beautiful little charm. A commotion ensued and an SS man intervened. The girl with the chain then realized that she was going to the gas chamber. A panic ensued, but it was very quickly contained. I did not think about this particular incident for so many years. I felt very guilty about it because it was I who first commented about the beauty of the charm. This was the only time I went to help out in this location so close to the gas chambers.

Chapter 18

TRANSPORTS FROM HUNGARY

IN 1944, THE TRANSPORTS of Jewish prisoners from Hungary started to arrive. Those of us who were assigned to register them were told that they were special transports slated for work camps, and that they were here only to be processed. They brought with them some of their most precious possessions, which were immediately taken away from them. They indeed received different treatment in processing than had been accorded to the rest of us. They were not shaved; nor were they tattooed for identification. They received gray dresses that were specially made for them, in contrast to the ragged clothing that had been given to us.

They only stayed with us for a brief period of time, and then they were sent to work camps. As it later turned out, this was, for me, a fortunate arrangement, and a turning point in my life.

They were told that they would be quarantined before they could join the civilians in the work camps.

During their two weeks of quarantine, they were housed in the same old filthy barracks in which we were. They received the same inadequate food that we did.

As Schreiberin, I took part in the registration procedure. At first, the women, overwhelmed and confused, asked all sorts of questions. The Germans offered fictitious answers to their inquiries. The new arrivals soon noticed flames billowing out of the five chimneys. Everybody was curious about the flames, and about the pervasive and nauseating stench. The Germans told them that the flames emanated from the bakeries. Having heard that, a young woman approached me and asked for a piece of bread. I said that it hadn't arrived yet, that it came only at specified hours, and would not be available until noon. When it finally came, precut into individual portions, one of the women complained that the ration was too small and wouldn't last the day as she was told it should. She wanted to know why she was not getting more, since there were five bakeries in full time operation. I told her these were not bakeries.

I eventually became irritated with the complaining woman and told her to shut up. Insulted, she told me that she was not really Jewish. She was married to an Aryan and what right did I, an Eastern European Jew, have to tell her what to do. She complained about me to the German overseer. Even though I had been there for a long time and knew many who were in charge, there were quite a few that I did not know. I was really scared. She told the guard a story of how she was married to a very important non-Jew. He told her, *"Aber dein Blut ist doch Jüdish."* "You are still a Jew." She did not like it, and let him know it. He pushed her with the butt of his gun. Thereafter she stopped complaining. I empathized with her even though she angered me.

For awhile I was afraid. I thought that the guard might hit or mistreat me. Once they started beating, no one knew where it would end. I once saw someone kicked. She hadn't stepped back far enough to allow the tormentor to pass. He hit her again; she fell and didn't get up fast enough so he kicked her to death there in the street. We were stunned but there was absolutely nothing we could do. Our helplessness filled us with an unrelenting inner rage. I don't know how we were able to contain ourselves.

Sometimes people who had intermarried or were only part Jewish would ask for special treatment. They did not know that all prisoners were treated in the same inhuman and degrading manner, but only the Jewish prisoners were candidates for the gas chambers.

In camp all Jews were treated badly; there was no such thing as better Jews. There was no difference between a peasant, a professor, or an artist. We were all equal. It took a great deal of strength and spirit to keep our heads above water. Because you were a Jew, the Germans could perpetrate all manner of bodily harm and degradations. Even animals are not treated so dastardly. It seems that our SS guards were always in a fulminating rage. It took very little to set them off. Quite often they needed no valid reason to explode, especially since the victims were always at hand.

At the begining of 1944 rumors spread, in all likelihood initiated by the underground, that the war was not going well for Germany and that our liberation by the Allies was imminent. We saw no signs of change until sometime late in the spring of 1944, when civilians began arriving in Auschwitz to select workers for factories. We heard that the German situation on all fronts was not good and that they tried to enlist more men into the service. We learned through the grapevine in the men's camp where people apparently had radios and knew exactly what was going on outside, that all German males holding so-called "soft" jobs were shipped to the fronts. It seems that more workers were needed in factories to replace the recently drafted men.

The recently arrived Hungarian women prisoners were put to work in these factories. From that point on, our camp became an abundant supplier of slave labor for factories.

Chapter 19

ESCAPE FROM AUSCHWITZ TO WORK CAMP IN CZECHOSLOVAKIA

SHORTLY AFTER THE HUNGARIAN transports settled in Birkenau, a number of civilian German men began making brief visits to our camp. As soon as they arrived, orders came from the front office that all the prisoners in transit to work camps should assemble in front of their barracks to await inspection by these visitors.

The initial order was that we assemble in rows of five, just as we did for a Zähl-appell. When the civilian men, accompanied by some highly placed officials from camp, arrived at the Block, one of the local officials directed everyone to disrobe, ostensibly to single out the prisoners who might be ill with typhus. It was a degrading and humiliating procedure. Disrobing for the German guards was distressing enough, but, after all, they were our oppressors and in our minds they were not men, not human beings; to do so for civilians felt absolutely unbearable, revolting. Unfortunately, there was no choice, for as soon as some of the women prisoners became restless and vocal with objections, the guards bore down on them, using their whips and physical force to restore order. It is important to note that these prisoners had arrived in Birkenau very recently and their experience in dealing with camp authority was very limited, especially when it came to avoiding becoming a target for their abuse.

As soon as order was restored, civilians, followed by the entourage of camp bigwigs, started moving between the rows of prisoners, occasionally picking some out of the rows and letting the Schreiberin know that this or that particular prisoner was not acceptable. There were not too many of these. The remaining prisoners were returned to the barracks to await the completion of the transaction. It was almost like a business transaction: the factory owners or directors needed a number of slave laborers, and they came to Birkenau where the order was filled.

The visits by civilians for the purpose of picking workers was repeated several times during the fall of 1944.

Some time after a group of workers were inspected, an official order from a specific factory was received in the main office. At this point, the secretary of the barracks was advised that there was a request for, let us say, two hundred factory workers. This meant that two hundred prisoners had to be prepared to be transferred out of Auschwitz. Just as when they entered camp, the prisoners slated for transfer received relatively fresh looking civilian clothing. On the day of departure, they showered, dressed, and assembled in front of the main office where the transaction was completed, that is, where the camp officials handed over to the civilian officials the number of prisoners that these particular civilians requested.

As the visits by the civilians started to diminish, I got the idea of smuggling myself out of Auschwitz with one of the groups that I had to prepare for the transfer out of camp. To me it seemed pretty simple. I got an order to prepare two hundred prisoners. I had many more in my Block than the number selected for work. Since the request did not specify exactly which individuals were to go (it just said two hundred prisoners), I decided to include myself among those to be shipped.

I broached my idea to the Blockälteste, the Verträterin, and a couple of secretaries and friends whom I trusted. I swore them to secrecy because if it was revealed, I would undoubtedly be shot. About six of us knew of my plan. Eventually, I involved another, a German-born prisoner who was a *Kapo,* or work-supervisor in camp. At first, they all thought that I was crazy. Slowly, I managed to convince some to help me. I was very much aware that I would be taking a great chance myself, in addition to endangering those who helped me. But all I could think of was that if it was true that the war would soon end, then whether Germany would be the winner or the loser, we, the old prisoners, would be blown up. I kept reminding my friends about what was in store for us, and eventually some agreed to help me. One, Emma, even decided to join me.

In response to the request for two hundred laborers, I submitted an alphabetical list of two hundred names to the main office, including Emma's name and mine. No identification numbers were required to be listed with the names. That list was to be used only to verify that in fact there were two hundred present for the roll call at the gate when leaving.

Only the most trusted and reliable friends could be involved in my plan. I had to work fast to convince those whom I selected to help me, as well as on purchasing suitable civilian clothing that I could take with me. My friends came through with flying colors. They purchased for me, with their bread rations and mine, a brownish beige tweed coat, a few skirts and blouses, a gray and maroon long cashmere sweater, a pair of shoes, stockings, and underwear. They even brought me a little watch. This outfit was not conspicuous, though I was attired a bit differently from the rest of the group; as Schreiberin I usually dressed a bit better than most. The others all wore serviceable civilian clothes that had been issued to them.

On the designated day, I dressed in my new finery. I assembled 199 women, including my friend Emma who had agreed to leave with me. The two hundreth place was taken by a very good friend of mine who was to stand in for me until the last moment. This completed the sum of two hundred workers requested by that order from the factory.

The Blockälteste, the Verträterin, and I, in the capacity of Schreiberin, marched with the contingent of two hundred prisoners from our Block to the gate located next to the front office. Accompanying us were my good friend, who was an important work supervisor (a Kapo) and two German guards charged with accompanying the group to the front office.

There I arranged my charges into forty rows of five prisoners in each row. My stand-in was in the thirty-ninth row, second from the end on the right side of the column. The other officials and I were all assembled on the left side of the column at the very beginning of the group. The Lagerälteste, accompanied by her German superior and two German officials unknown to us who had just arrived with the assignment to accompany our group on the trip to our destination, reviewed the list of prisoners that were being transferred.

The Lagerälteste, her supervisor, and I went down the column to confirm that the count was correct, and that the prisoners looked presentable. This done, all of us returned to the gate. The transaction completed, an order was given by the German official in charge of our camp to open the gate, and our column started moving out of the gate.

Under the pretext that the column was not marching straight, I left the group of officials in front and started working my way to the back of the column, straightening the lines, reprimanding the marchers to walk erect, all in a loud voice so as to be heard by the officials in front. As the end of the column came closer to the gate, I went around to the right side, and changed places with my friend who had been standing in for me. She slipped out as I stepped in.

Before I knew it, we passed the gate, and I heard the noise of the closing of the gate behind us.

We were loaded onto a freight train, and a short while later the train moved away from Birkenau.

My heart pounded, but I was walking on air. I still wasn't sure that they would not come after me once I entered the train. We were marched into a cattle car and started off. I don't think I was able to eat anything that day. When we sat in that dark and airless place, I felt a little hungry but I didn't consider that so important. I didn't unwind until we arrived in the new camp. We traveled for what seemed an eternity. I had not come to Auschwitz by train; I came in a truck and traveled a shorter distance at that time. But the difference now was that we stopped at designated points where we were fed, and they allowed us to go to the latrine outside. I was excited and fearful. I did not know what to expect.

I left Birkenau in November 1944.

I do not know what happened after I left. I have no idea if anyone ever tried an escape similar to me. In Stockholm, I met several Czech women whom I had known to be Blockälteste in Birkenau. They assured me that my scheme was never discovered. Thus none of my friends who helped me suffered on my account.

I had been interned in Auschwitz for almost two years. When I first broached my plan to leave to my friends, they didn't think that I would succeed. But I did. The fact that Emma accompanied me made my efforts a little easier, because all of the others were strangers. That isolation didn't last very long.

During the trip, we learned that we were on our way to Czechoslovakia, actually to Sudeten Germany. We arrived in a town called Oberaltstadt, for which the Czechoslovakian name is *Stare Mesto, Nad Wahom*. It was located in the mountains and the camp proper was located a short distance from the town. It was a work camp. The barracks were different; they were made of wood and contained individual rooms. We slept in bunk beds, ten women in a room. Each of us was given a separate bed. The people in the barracks next to ours came from many and varied cities and towns. They asked us, the new arrivals, a great many questions. However, they were probably better informed than we were. We were delighted to be there. To us it was luxurious. There was a dining room. The food though was slop, not very palatable, but there were potatoes that were surprisingly edible, and soup that was passable. There was a main camp, but we were sent to a newer division, a few miles from the old one.

Our camp consisted of only one or two barracks just for those of us who were newly arrived. A washroom was also available. And a fairly nice toilet, not a latrine. We spent one day just getting acclimated. The camp was supervised by two women and one or two men, all from the SS guard. This was a satellite camp.

I don't remember the name of the main camp. There were many barracks in the main camp where we would eat our main meals. A day or two after our arrival we learned that we would be working in a factory that served the military. We had somehow suspected this.

The main camp had different work assignments to accommodate the many factories in the area. We were surrounded by mountains which hid the factories nestled in a valley.

The factory to which we were assigned produced a variety of small parts for airplanes. We had very little contact with the outside world, except sometimes at night. We alternated day and night shifts with civilian French workmen.

It was November, and extremely cold. We rose at about four or five o'clock to have some ersatz coffee and a piece of bread. Then we marched to the workplace. It took a long time to reach it because the factory was a long distance from our camp. I remember few details about the actual camp or about the town. I do recall walking through the small towns in Czechoslovakia where people regarded us with curiosity and suspicion. Every once in a while someone would approach the outside row of our column and offer us an apple or some other small item. People would sometimes stop to talk with us, but we were forbidden to talk with anybody. When we walked into the factory, the doors were locked behind us and we lost all contact with the outside world. Every so often they would ask some of us to deliver a finished part to a different part of the factory. Very special workers were selected for this task, which involved leaving one's working area.

Once I was asked to bring some special pieces from another division. They were large trays stacked with various parts, some made of aluminum, some of iron, and others of lead. It was a heavy load and I barely made it to my floor. Recently x-rays have shown an old injury to my rib cage. I can attribute it only to this experience.

I used to work on a machine that drilled holes in various aluminum airplane parts. The machine resembled an upright piano. It was equipped with grooves instead of keys in which we placed the part with which we worked. Our drill press reminded me of a soda fountain. It took a long time before we learned how to use this tool effectively.

At one point, I decided that perhaps the machines didn't break down frequently enough. So I would cut the belt. Of course, it had to be done at night when the male supervisor was off in a far corner, sleeping or fraternizing with the women guards. When the belt broke, there was a loud snap that scared people because it sounded like an explosion. After a while they began to wonder why the accident happened only on my machine. Sometimes I would cut the belts on someone else's machine. It didn't take much effort to accomplish this. It was partly sabotage, and partly because we needed the leather. We used it for soles in our shoes, which were worn paper-thin. We devised many ways of sewing the leather onto the shoes. Soon, all the leather belts in the machines were replaced with rubberized cloth.

During the day, matters grew very tense because the guards rushed us to fulfill their quotas. After a while we noticed that some of the parts we made were being returned, ostensibly for minor repairs. We became suspicious and started to investigate in our own way. We questioned the supervisors and the French workers. It was difficult for me since I couldn't speak French. We managed to communicate, using our hands and relying on the little German they spoke. From the French workers we learned that the Germans were cut off from Berlin and therefore were not able to send the material we needed. Actually we were making the same things over and over again. We were doing "busy work."

There was one supervisor, Engel, who must have been a sick man since he was not called for service in the army. He apparently came from a very small town. He told me that he had never seen a Jew before. He saw pictures of Jews only in the Nazi paper, *Der Stürmer*. There the Jew was depicted as the devil incarnate with horns, a crooked nose, and curly hair. He was distressed to discover, upon seeing us, that we looked different from the stereotype. He was upset when he saw some prisoners fighting for food, or scraping the emptied soup container with their bare hands. Some of the prisoners were hefty women and the portions of food we received were not really enough, and when it was cold, they craved hot soup. He couldn't understand how some of the women would literally crawl into that huge receptacle to scoop the soup out with their fingers, their tongues, or with whatever tools they had. That is how desperately hungry we were.

Engel would pass by my machine and mutter, "How can they act like that, like animals?" He couldn't understand and I was loath to discuss the subject with him. He was afraid of being caught talking to one person at great length; he would sneak over to my machine and start a conversation.

One night, while drilling, I whistled music by Mozart. Engel kept circling around me as if something untoward had happened. I wondered what he wanted. I finally asked what was the matter.

He looked at me challengingly and said. "I just want to know whether you know what you're whistling." I said, "Yes," and I named the piece.

He said, "How do you know it?"

I said, "I wasn't born in a forest, I am an educated person."

He did not think that Jews knew anything about classical music or about literature. From that time on, he tried to be friendly.

He still didn't come to my machine that often. If he knew that the food had arrived (sometimes it was left outside), he would stand with me in the front so that I would be served first and wouldn't have to push along with everybody else. These were favors that I really didn't need, but I didn't want to antagonize him. The German SS men and SS women were more difficult than the civilians were.

Engel was the one who later told me that Berlin was cut off. With the isolation of Berlin, the Germans had serious problems.

But to us the guards complained incessantly about the rationing of salt. We didn't care whether we had salt or not, as long as we had food. I believe the salt issue was just a smoke screen, an excuse, because there were salt mines in Czechoslovakia and Poland. Perhaps there were no trains available for shipping materials to us, or maybe they were using the trains for other purposes. We were aware that fewer deliveries were being made to our factory.

One day Engel said, "How can you eat without salt?" I replied that I didn't care whether or not I had it as long as I had something to eat. He promised to bring me some salt the next day. He waited till we worked the nightshift before he kept his promise. To play it safe, he wrapped a pinch of salt in a huge newspaper. He then left the package on top of a garbage pail. I never picked it up. He was rather unsophisticated. He often wanted to know what he could do for me but unfortunately he was in no position to help. He had no authority to take me away from my work. Besides I became quite efficient in operating my machine.

We continued to work in the factory till mid-April of 1945.

Chapter 20

END OF THE WAR

ONE APRIL MORNING as we were marching through town, two young men brushed against us to let us know in a whisper that Franklin Roosevelt had died and that there was a new President in the United States. We didn't know how it would affect us.

In the beginning of May, the Czechs told us that Hitler had died. They didn't say how. As we marched through the town, we noticed that every window displayed Hitler's picture draped in black. To us it was truly a wish come true, yet we were apprehensive. The following day the Germans ordered all of us out of the factory and marched us out into the fields. They told us that we had to perform an important task. We were to dig trenches because they anticipated that the Russian and British tanks were headed in our direction. This was the first time that I knew that the Russians were fighting the Germans. The trenches would stall the tanks. For two or three days we were taken into those large fields to dig trenches.

The meadows in which we were working were surrounded by forests at a distance. We talked among ourselves, trying to decide whether we should make a run for the trees. I was opposed to this plan. If I attempted it, the dogs and the Germans could easily overtake me because the field before the forest was wide open. The Germans were talking with a degree of irritation we had never noticed before. I told the girls that I was not going to run and those who wished to do so should make their own decision. One girl who opted to run was shot to death.

On our third day in the field we noticed that our guards were no longer watching us. Instead they were engaged in what appeared to be a very animated discussion. We knew immediately that something unusual was happening. Someone remarked, "Look at that, they are over there and are not even looking in our direction."

They brought us our lunch and after we finished, they ordered us to assemble in marching formation. They told us that we were returning to camp. Now we were certain that something was going on. It was obvious that they didn't know what to do, that further orders hadn't come through. They brought us to the main camp, the place of our original arrival. The camp was as busy as a beehive. Everyone was running around. The whispered word was that the war was over. But the Germans were still around. We noticed that one of the mounds, under which the potatoes were buried for the winter, was open and prisoners were stuffing potatoes into their pockets. The Germans were too preoccupied to pay any attention to this activity. There was so much happening.

We returned to our camp. We had *Abendbrot*—coffee and bread for the evening. We all huddled, thinking that the atmosphere wasn't really right. Finally the Kommandant, the lady in charge, entered and ordered: "Lights out!" And we had to go to bed. She left and the doors were closed. There were five double bunks and ten occupants in our room. We tried to sleep, but we were very excited. We knew that something important was happening.

At dawn, someone who went to the bathroom came back screaming: "The Germans are gone!" We all ran out in our nightgowns, looked around, and confirmed that there was no one there. The screams were loud and prolonged. We couldn't wait for the skies to brighten. We hugged and kissed. We knew that if we were alone, the war was over.

We didn't know what to do. We wanted to break up the camp, but I restrained everyone. They respected me and listened to what I had to say. I cautioned, "Look, we don't know how long we are going to be here; let's not raze the place. We still have to live somewhere and right now we don't know where to go. Let's remain until the morning at least." We waited patiently but no one came. We sat there still confused about what to do.

Some ventured out into the town. One of the girls, a big strong peasant type, walked into town and came back later with two or three British POWs in tow. There were such camps all around our camp. No one could speak English, but they came to me because they thought I could. Before the war, when we were planning to go to Australia, I had attended the Berlitz school for a few weeks to study English. I learned how to say "Hello," "How are you?" Finally two girls persuaded me to speak with the Englishmen. They in turn were eager to communicate with us to tell us that the war was over. It seems that they too were abandoned by their guards. So we asked who was going to liberate us. We were all hoping that it would be the Americans or the English, rather than the Russians. They told us that no decision has been reached; that our town was just a small "hole in the wall."

After we screamed through half the night, I lay down on my bed, and that was when I started to think about my mother, how I had survived, and where I was going. This brought on a deep depression.

Two days later, in the middle of a sunny day someone entered my room to tell me that somebody was looking for me.

It was Engel, "They told me that you are in charge."

I said, "This is not so. They consult with me, but by and large they all do as they please." He told me that he was afraid of being punished and wanted me to protect him.

I said, "You are a civilian. You were just working here. There is very little help I can offer." He continued to plead.

Finally I told him, "Get out, because if you are seen here, I am not responsible for what they might do."

He was scared. He remembered a conversation we had one night when I was working on the drilling machine. He was assuming that the war would be over soon and he wanted to know how I would punish the Germans who treated me so badly. I told him that I would round up all the German males, line them up in front of my machine, and render them permanently incapable of reproducing another "superior race."

He thought I was terrible, "How could you say a thing like that?"

I continued, "I would then confine them to camps similar to the ones in which we were kept."

As he now begged for his life, he was very frightened and concerned only about himself. He asked, "You are not going to do anything to me?"

I said: "No, but I have no sympathy for you or yours."

"But," he reminded me, "I was so nice to you."

"Yes, you gave me salt and put it in the garbage can." I finally told him, "I really cannot do anything for you, but I will not harm you, so just leave."

He did, and I never saw him again.

LIBERATION, READJUSTMENT, AND EXPLORATION

FOLLOWING THE ANNOUNCEMENT that the war was over, there were a couple of hours of complete chaos. People ran around our little camp aimlessly, not knowing what to do or where to go. They roamed the area in utter disbelief, expecting that at any moment the guards would appear again. The mood changed as time passed and as people ventured out to the little town. They started by walking small distances, and then longer ones. Our newfound freedom imbued us with a mixture of euphoria, anger, and aggression. After exploring the town, some of our women would force their way into civilian homes and official storage depots. From there they would expropriate all food, clothing, and other essentials. Some prisoners went hunting for the German men and women who were in charge of our small camp. Some were more successful than others and brought back some of the guards. They put them to work cleaning toilets. One of the captured guards had a freshly tattooed number on her forearm. She was obviously trying to save herself by posing as a liberated concentration camp prisoner.

We had a couple of casualties because of the sudden and uncontrolled access to food. Lots of raw meat was brought into our camp. Having gone without proper food for a long time, people grabbed any edible they could find regardless of whether it was suitable for eating, even though there was no place to cook it. Someone soon devised a method by which we would place a small piece of meat over a fire between two bricks, but it wasn't clean, nor could we wait for the meat to get done. We lost several people because of this; people reacted to the sudden plethora of food in a completely irrational manner. There was no way to persuade them that it could be dangerous to eat half-raw food. It was a painful experience to lose three or four women from our camp. Although we warned and cautioned them beforehand, it was still horrible to stand by helplessly as they writhed and died from severe cramps induced by overeating, just days after they regained their freedom. As the gorging continued, a few of us admonished our people, advising them not to eat too much or too fast. Since it was the beginning of May, the meat was probably spoiling as it lay exposed to the sun.

During the day, the prisoners foraged all over the place trying to find things. Some broke into people's homes. Not all of the local inhabitants had sided with the Germans, but some reportedly did. In our eagerness to punish the collaborators, I think we harmed people who weren't involved. I make no apology; strictly speaking, everybody was involved, even those who did nothing but sit back and watch unconcernedly. Some of the town's residents pleaded with us not to be wild and unkind. But there was no rationale for such leniency. I remember exactly how I felt. I couldn't run into the city to do what others did, but neither could I condemn them. I said, "If you can seize a German, more power to you." Those prisoners who participated in raiding civilian homes were able to release some of their repressed anger. I kept mine inside. Strangely, I was depressed after liberation.

For a couple of days, our area was no-man's-land. We didn't know who was going to take over. We were already aware that the Allies had divided parts of southern Germany. We all prayed that we would be under the jurisdiction of England or America but eventually we learned that the Russians would administer our territory. On the day the Russian army marched into Oberaltstadt, we were all out to greet them.

When we watched the Russian army march into Oberaltstadt, they actually rolled in on the tops of tanks, looking victorious. All of them had their sleeves rolled up, displaying with pride rows of watches on each arm. I had a little timepiece that I brought with me from Auschwitz. On the second day I was walking in a street of that little town where our camp was located, a soldier noticed me, examined my watch, and appropriated it. I asked, "What do you need it for?" He had about five watches on each arm. He said, "We have many men's watches, big ones, and I need a small one. I want yours." I was very angry.

The Russian soldiers didn't go out of their way to hit us, but they certainly demonstrated no genuine sympathy.

When the Russians moved into Oberaltstadt, I met a high-ranking Russian officer named Levine. He visited our camp, sat with us for a couple of hours and listened to our stories. He seemed moved but never offered us anything concrete (food, for instance). He was rather ambivalent about exhibiting any sympathy lest he be accused of being Jewish first and not Russian. A trait that offended me was the reluctance of many officers to acknowledge in any way that they were Jewish.

The day after the Russians arrived, they also started searching for Nazi collaborators. After they rounded up all the Germans, they wouldn't allow us near them. Instead, the Russians loaded their prisoners on trucks, purportedly for deportation to Siberia. We felt that the Nazis were getting off too easily. We wanted to see something more tangible, some immediate punishment. Angrily, we tried to stone the Germans as they were being loaded onto the trucks. The Russian soldiers just stood there, and formed a barricade to keep us away. It is true that we were wild and tried to get our hands on some of them, especially those we knew. It wasn't only the collaborators. There were also Nazis who had been hiding in our area. We complained to the Russians and were told that the Germans would be sent into prisons and held for trials in Germany, before their deportation to Russia. We really didn't believe that they were going to do either.

We learned that our area would be controlled by the Russians, but none of us wanted to live under that regime. Shortly after they took over, we met a couple of Czech partisans, and made arrangements for them to try to get us out of the area. They hoped to get two jeeps, but they were able to get only one.

One evening our new-found friends offered to drive four of us early the following morning to a major railroad station where we could board a train for Prague. It was a very difficult decision to make. There were two hundred in our immediate group from Auschwitz; who would go and who would be left behind? I really don't remember, at this point, how it was decided, but it was all very hush-hush. I was selected as one of the four to be moved out. We packed in a hurry. I owned a long gray and maroon cashmere sweater, also a good woolen coat all bought in Auschwitz. At this time in May warm clothes were no longer needed. Besides, we had received uniforms when we arrived in this camp. Now I wore my own clothing. For this trip, I repacked everything under the lining of the coat because it was easier to carry that way instead of lugging a bundle.

When we reached the station, there was no train. Instead we saw a sea of people, probably from the neighboring camps. If it were not for those five Czechs, who apparently had connections, we would not have been able to get tickets or to board the train, which arrived after a long delay. There was a great deal of pushing and shoving. Everyone wanted to return to Poland. Shortly after the train left the station, it screeched to a stop. There seemed to be something wrong, but no one knew what. The four of us sat together. We took turns checking when the train would move. After a while we were asked to get off. All those with tickets gathered in one place. At one point, I left two of the girls to watch our packages and accompanied the other one to find out what was happening. Somebody said the train would leave in an hour. Another heard that the train would not leave until the next day.

When I returned to our group, I noticed that the two girls whom we left behind to mind our things were quite busy talking with some people. I looked for our packages and my coat as well as a small notebook, but they were gone. I was upset, but not for long. I was left with only what I wore and what I was carrying in my hand. Months later I met an old friend who was sure that I had been killed when she saw someone else wearing my cashmere sweater.

Eventually we boarded the train and it started inching along. At one point the train stopped and once again we were told to get out. We were informed that the tracks ahead were broken and that we couldn't move any further. We also learned that we were about fifteen kilometers from Morawska Ostrava. They didn't know when the tracks would be repaired but we decided that a distance of fifteen kilometers was not too difficult to negotiate, so we all started to march to Morawska Ostrava. Several hundreds of us walked. We looked like a procession of weary pilgrims. Some carried packages, others had nothing. Morawska Ostrava is a large city in Czechoslovakia. Some of the girls who had robbed homes near the camp in the days following our liberations amassed some valuables which they later used to trade for what they needed. I had no money or other assets, but I was not worried. I had my freedom.

As we approached the outskirts of Morawska Ostrava, many of the Czechs stood in front of their homes with large pots of soup, welcoming us and ladling out the hot nourishing liquid as we passed their houses. It was a moving moment. Most of these people seemed to belong to the lower economic class. The soups were plain potato and a little barley, but to us, they couldn't have tasted better. Eventually we arrived at a central point, where we found organized activity. We were registered and assigned lodgings in various places.

The four of us were sent to a beautiful hotel located in the center of town. I cannot adequately describe our reaction to the hotel room. It contained a huge double bed. No pillows, just a big feather bed quilt without linen on the mattress or the cover. We were elated; we jumped and cavorted on that bed like children. That was 1945. I was already twenty-five years old, but I felt and behaved like a child. All four of us slept in that one bed. In return for our lodgings in the hotel, we were assigned to peel potatoes in the kitchen for a couple of hours a day. We took our meals in a designated hotel room.

We had a great deal of free time to walk around town to sightsee and perhaps find people whom we knew. After a day or so, we met two young men who I thought were officers in the British Army. I thought also that they were POWs. They said they were of Polish descent and had families in Poland; they planned to go back there to try to find people they knew. One had a mother and the other a couple of sisters or aunts and uncles in Poland. We were struck by the lucky coincidence that they were going to Poland. We had met them several times in the main UNRRA[27] station where we were all wandering about asking questions. The Britishers finally decided to try to requisition a car. If they could get gasoline, they could take two of us back to Cracow.

Cracow suited me fine. I hoped that the Loho family would permit me to stay with them for a while. We started for Cracow about a week later. After driving for ten miles we were stopped at a checkpoint. Two fat Russians emerged from a makeshift office and asked, "Who are you and where are you going?" They led us into their office and asked a number of rather unexpected questions. They wanted to see our identification papers. When the Russians interrogated us, they were really very mean. Some of the fear that we lost when the war ended suddenly returned.

I have a rather prominent number tattooed on my left forearm, but that meant nothing to them. They said, "You could have had it put on recently; all the Germans are doing it." I tried to explain my situation to them in the best way I could. I don't speak Russian, but I could converse in Polish and German, and they could talk German. I explained that a new tattoo looks different than an old one, and as an experienced officer he should know that mine was not a newly acquired tattoo. They were really suspicious. After screaming and marching us into another room, they interviewed us individually and jointly. Obviously our Russian interrogators did not believe that we were concentration camp survivors; therefore they decided to remand two of us to jail.

A young Czech soldier was assigned to escort me and my friend to the city's main prison. During our walk, I tried to prevail upon the guard not to turn us over to the prison authorities. I played on his sympathy, recounting what had happened to me, where I had been and my present destination. I pointed out that no one would know the difference if he let me go. I asked if he had some document for me to sign. If so, I would do so. I assured him that the man who sent him with us would be drunk by tomorrow and wouldn't even remember what happened today. He remained quiet. Eventually he brought us into town. Apparently I succeeded in touching a sympathetic chord in this young man. I scrawled a signature on the paper he was supposed to return and he released us.

In town, we went back to the central office. I reported what had happened. They gave me a paper containing identifying information, and a statement that confirmed that we were returning from Auschwitz and that asked people to be as courteous and as helpful as possible. It also affirmed that we were Jewish; at that time, this was supposedly no longer a hindrance. I kept that document and even-

27. United Nations Relief and Rehabilitation Association

tually donated it along with other papers from that period to YIVO.[28] With this certificate we were reassigned to the hotel in which we had previously stayed.

A day or so later, I went to the main office where everyone congregated, and I was pleasantly surprised to see the two Englishmen again. In answer to my inquiry, they asked me to forget what had happened. They now knew how to get out of town without encountering any checkpoints. They also were able to get their papers in order (apparently they obtained some false documents). They said, "Girls, if you want to return, the offer still stands!" The next day four of us got into a car and started on our journey to Cracow: to Poland once again. It was a very long trip. We ran out of gas, and came upon roads with congested traffic. There were checkpoints at the Czechoslovakian border where they examined our papers. Never again did we encounter any unpleasantness from officials. Usually, they quickly looked over the documents we presented and allowed us to continue on our way. In some places, we ran into more difficulty than in others, but we were never detained. That arrest at the first checkpoint had depressed all of us, and even though we made light of the experience, we were all wary, never knowing when it could happen again. We did finally get to Cracow and there we parted. The two men were continuing east. We didn't exchange names. My girl companion stayed in Cracow for awhile, and then went on to her hometown. I couldn't have traveled any further; I just wanted to rest and find out what I could do in Cracow.

In this rather large city of Cracow we found a shelter for returnees from concentration camps supervised by the United Nations Relief and Rehabilitation Association or it might have been the Joint Distribution Committee. We registered and were told that their lists were sent to America once a week, by courier. I told them that my father and two uncles lived in Brooklyn, New York.

I was skeptical that these lists would actually reach my family, but I continued to hope. This shelter contained many bunk beds, too many per room, and though it wasn't a prison, it looked worse than the last camp in which I had been, where we had separate rooms with a few bunks in each.

When we arrived in Cracow, we learned that all of Poland was under Russian rule. I never wanted to live under Russian domination, mainly because I believed that one totalitarian state is no different from any other.

There were always a great many people from different towns and walks of life at the Cracow main refugee office. We were not too easy to deal with. The world owed us everything. Some were angry and nothing was good enough for them.

---

28. YIVO Institute for Jewish Research, currently the main center outside Israel for Yiddish studies

There were crowds of people waiting for their assignments of living quarters, food, clothing, and jobs. Some were understandably intolerant of their new circumstances. Others were happy and thankful that they had survived. We all looked for someone we knew. Eventually, I was given a bed. The room resembled a huge depot crowded with bunk beds and people. Each one was preoccupied with his own problems.

The day after my arrival, I decided that I would look for the Loho family with whom I had lived prior to my arrest. The Lohos were delighted to see me, especially the children. They asked many questions and I was invited to stay for dinner, meager as it would be. I was welcomed as if I were a long lost relative. I described my situation to them, as well as the central shelter. The Lohos immediately started to think about getting me out of there by finding a job for me. Mrs. Loho's daughter, a roentgenologist, promised that she would inquire about employment at the hospital.

True to her word, on the following day she told me that there was a young doctor whose wife had died in childbirth. He had moved back with his mother who needed help with the care of the infant. This job would furnish me with living quarters, a room for myself, and a small salary. Since the responsibility for the baby's welfare would be shared by me and the grandmother, I accepted the position. The doctor was fairly well-to-do. He had a nice, big apartment. There was a room for me, and both he and his mother were fairly kind to me. After a while I found working there emotionally stressful because I was faced with a situation of living with a family yet not having one of my own. The grandmother was a cold and remote woman. It was a job. I couldn't really blame anyone, and I was grateful to be out of the shelter. I was glad that my employment was not far from the Lohos, so that I could visit them often. During the day I was occupied with the child.

As I adjusted to my duties and relaxed, I tried to find out whether anyone knew anything about my mother or the rest of my family. I was unsuccessful, I was too far removed from Chelm. Finally I decided that the job was not for me. I realized that I did not want to remain in Cracow or in this kind of job.

While I was working there, my Uncle Avrom Globen found his way back to Chelm. He learned that I had survived and wrote to me. I had previously corresponded with an old Polish neighbor in Chelm to find out who had come back. I learned that Masha, one of my schoolmates from gimnazium had returned and had a small apartment of her own. In fact, she urged me to come to Chelm, but there was really nothing there for me. I received this letter from my Uncle Avrom, (my father's youngest sister's husband, the only member of our family, who had survived in Russia) he suggested that I come back to Chelm. I decided to do so. He had an ulterior motive. He was interested in getting back my grandmother's house and the bakery that his wife once operated with her mother. I didn't own any property because my parents had sold everything before we left. My grandmother's property was taken over by the Poles. My uncle wanted me to return so that together we could try to retrieve what was once ours. I was not particularly interested, but I still wanted to get closer to Chelm; I might find my mother or others who might know what happened to her.

I eventually met a young woman who told me that she saw my mother in Majdanek, a concentration camp near Lublin. She said she saw my mother die, probably of hunger, because she was quite swollen. When she fell, someone found twenty zloty in her pocket, which she was apparently saving for an emergency.

RETURN TO CHELM

I RETURNED TO CHELM and moved in with Masha, my old schoolmate. For some time her home served as headquarters for all of our surviving friends. She survived the war as an Aryan. She was handicapped with a club foot. Throughout the war she was a tutor, and she lived and carried on her work as a non-Jew. Masha's place wasn't really adequate. Her apartment was a huge room located in an attic. Her furnishings consisted of a straw mattress on the floor, a table and two chairs. She continued to tutor children in their homes. She would receive some money and food for her fee. Sometimes she would bring home part of her meal for me.

There was no running water in Masha's attic. It was my chore to carry home two pails of water from a street pump located around the corner. I don't know how she managed when I was not there, but somehow she did. I also cleaned and managed what little food we had.

I had no money and my uncle kept urging me to fight for the return of my grandmother's property. He could not do so officially because he was not a Berland. I had mixed feelings about this endeavor and decided not to sign the required papers. The last thing in the world that I wanted was to get involved with the Polish authorities in a long drawn-out battle to recover property. It was too soon after we returned home from the camps. At that point, possessions meant very little to me, and I did not care whether my uncle succeeded in getting back the property. I wanted no part of the deal.

In Chelm, my birthplace where I was raised and schooled, Polish people who knew me were unpleasant. Few ever said, "I am glad that you survived." They would only ask, "How did you survive?" meaning, "What did you have to do to stay alive?"

At that time, rumors were rife that those who survived must have done something evil, used or killed somebody, or more likely collaborated with the Gestapo to ensure their survival. That kind of innuendo was terribly painful for me. Only one non-Jewish friend from school invited me to his home for dinner. It was a meager meal, but it was a shared one. Generally though, there was no renewal of old acquaintanceships. My Polish friends, old neighbors, and people whom I had known since my childhood days were reserved, distant, and rather cold. Since many of the Poles appropriated Jewish properties after we were deported, our return made them uncomfortable.

One afternoon, a couple of us visited the sister of one of my old classmates who had not survived. We gathered on their balcony facing the main street to reminisce about old times. As we sat there, a few Polish hoodlums started to shoot at us from across the street. They used real bullets, and cursed us. One of them yelled in Polish, "Jews go back to Palestine!" This was an old taunt; we heard it often while we were at school. We were terrified. We went to the police who made excuses for the offenders. "They are young, they are drunk." The police did nothing about our complaints.

Sometime during that summer, another school friend of ours, Paula, together with her boyfriend Herman came to Chelm, also looking for her family. They moved in with us. It was fun being together once more, recalling old times and talking about current ones. We laughed and cried. We wept because we were alive. My friend and her sister Guta had survived. Her parents did not. One evening, Paula told me, "There is no future for you in Chelm. You should settle in a larger city, where you could continue your schooling." She invited me to stay with her in Lodz. She planned to marry Herman shortly. By the end of the summer, they would have an apartment and I could move in with them. It was strange how eager we were to share all that we had. I packed all my belongings and left for Lodz a week or so later.

Masha remained in Chelm, because she had a job and could maintain herself. I hated to leave her but I had to. Paula and her husband opened a store in Lodz. She had also invited an uncle and his two young children to share her apartment. The family had survived because they had been hidden by some Poles in their small cellar. They spent months crouching a great deal of the time in cramped quarters. The people gave them food and the father and children would emerge at night to take care of their needs. When the war was over, the children could not stand straight. They had to be hospitalized because their joints were locked into a bent position. By the time I came to live with them, they were feeling better and were running around. It was a railroad flat consisting of two bedrooms, a living room, kitchen and bathroom, and a small entrance hall. The last bedroom was occupied by Paula and her husband. The middle one housed the uncle, his lady friend, and his children. The sitting-room contained a bed for me and one for Paula's younger sister, Guta. A couple of months later, another man came to live with us, so they set up a bed for him in the kitchen, and another one in the hall for anyone else who might wander in. The apartment was at a central point, where everybody, my friends, Paula's, or Herman's used to come for temporary shelter.

This place became another gathering center for people from Chelm or Rejowiec, Paula's hometown. People from Herman's hometown were also welcome.

LODZ: MAKING
NEW PLANS

I STARTED LOOKING into the possibility of enrolling at the university. I had a difficult time because I was Jewish and not a member of the Communist Party. I was interested in law, medicine, or architecture. I applied to several universities but I was given a runaround. One day, as I was returning from one of those interviews, I noticed a familiar looking girl on the other side of the street. When I got closer I recognized her as Gina, the youngest of the three sisters I had helped in Auschwitz, the one I had pulled out when she was selected for Block 25. I called her name, and she responded jubilantly. There I was, standing on one side of the street, with moving traffic between us and she on the other side with a big, white goose under her arm. I can still see it. She, the goose, and I ran towards each other. We embraced in the middle of the street, the traffic notwithstanding. We cried, hugged, and kissed and she told me that all three sisters had been moved from Birkenau and had survived Bergen-Belsen. They were now back in Lodz, under assumed non-Jewish names. They found that posing as Poles made it easier to get living quarters and anything else they needed or wanted.

They had a huge, beautiful apartment. Gina went to school but also served as the cook, cleaner, and housekeeper. The two other sisters were employed. The oldest of these, Tania, worked for a highly placed official in the Polish government. Her job carried with it many privileges. Our reunion was joyous; the screaming and merrymaking could probably be heard for miles. They suggested that I move in with them since they had a huge apartment. They had an uncle Alexander who had survived, a marvelous gentleman, who owned the apartment. We all became family. I called him "Uncle" and I was like another niece to him.

I did not move in. I stayed with Paula who had been a friend before the war, and with whom I felt quite comfortable. Tania exerted a lot of influence and obtained a job for me in a factory where I later became a supervisor. There was a great deal of discontent when I reported for work because I wasn't promoted from the ranks and I was not a party member, also probably because I was better educated than the rest of them, and most of all because I was a Jew. I could handle the job; after a while I was able to find a niche for myself in that place.

It was the fall of 1945, I had been unsuccessfully trying to get in touch with my father in New York. Unexpectedly, I received a letter from him, in which he wrote that he had heard about me on the radio. After the publication in the U.S. of the list of survivors compiled after I arrived in Cracow, a townsman learned from the radio that Felicia Berland from Chelm had survived and was now in Cracow. He called my uncle, and he in turn contacted my father, who was very excited. He immediately noticed that my mother's name was not mentioned. When it was learned that she had not survived, he suffered his first heart attack.

My father was happy to have found me and asked me to let him know what had happened to my mother. Everybody was envious. I was the lucky one who had a father in the United States.

I started to make plans to go to the United States. I encountered tremendous difficulties because at the time there was no American embassy in Poland. The recently appointed consul could not process emigration papers. One day I was informed that perhaps the consular officials could do something for me on the basis of the exit visa I had received in July of 1939. I boarded a train and called on the people in Chelm with whom I once left my fur coat. My papers and passport were also there. I retrieved the documents and traveled back to Lodz, but en route we had to change trains, and were delayed by a layover of several hours. As I sat in the station waiting, I fell asleep and when I woke, my passport and papers were gone. Someone had stolen them. This time it really happened!

I remember rising early that morning, seeing the sky, the trees, and hearing the birds. It was the first time that I was really able to enjoy the wonders of nature. For the longest time, though, I was depressed. Meeting and being among my friends buoyed my spirits. Nevertheless, the weariness remained with me for a very long time, even though on the surface it was not apparent.

I came back after this very strenuous trip of two days and nights in old trains without a passport, and had to start all over again. I returned to Warsaw where I was told it would take another year or more before an American embassy would be established in Poland.

I had the feeling, even though the Poles were running their country, that the Russians were in charge and they just didn't want to make it easy for anyone to leave. I kept writing to my father.

In the meantime, the middle one of the three sisters, Lusia, had met a fine young man who was doing very well financially. He had a very successful business. He was quite bright and aggressive. At first Lusia didn't think he was handsome enough for her. She was a beautiful girl. She resisted, but he persisted. Eventually he won her over because he was devoted and very much in love with her.

On Christmas Day, 1945 they were married. We were all very busy cooking, baking, and running around in circles. One evening one of the sisters and I returned to the apartment after work. As we climbed to the second floor, we heard a commotion and we saw things falling from the upper floor. It turned out that the prospective groom had ordered first quality poultry and instead was given second quality. He was so angry that he threw those chickens down after the delivery man. That night we laughed and cried. Some people had no food at all and here he was throwing out fairly good looking chickens.

On the evening before the wedding, the groom-to-be hired people to do our hair and nails. We all had facials and manicures. Suddenly we smelled something burning. It seems that we the cooks were busy having our hair done, and forgot to take the tongues out of the oven. The chief rabbi of the Polish Army officiated at the wedding. It was the first real *simcha*[29] in which we participated after the war.

At one point soon after their betrothal, Lusia's husband began talking about leaving Poland for Germany, from where it was reportedly easier to emigrate to America. He wanted to go to the German DP[30] camps from where it was quite easy for the survivors to get American visas. I wrote about this to my father who was adamantly opposed to my returning to German camps. He thought that I had had my fill of them. I was not eager to go there, but I couldn't stay in Poland either. I knew that the establishment of the embassy in Warsaw was a long way off. Somebody told me that it was easier to get to the United States from Sweden. This was a possibility worth exploring.

In the meantime I had moved out of Paula's house because a young man, a friend of Paula's husband, had moved in and begun to pursue me rather aggressively. I didn't feel safe there. Every night I had to fight him off. I didn't want to wake anyone or complain to my friends. Once I screamed and alarmed everyone. They thought it was very funny. I didn't. Besides he wasn't really my kind of man.

I knew of another girl from Chelm who survived as an Aryan and lived in a one-room apartment with her brother. When I told her the story, she said, "What do you mean? You have suffered enough, why do you have to continue to do so? Move in with me." I accepted her kind offer and lived there until I left for Sweden. Her name was Blumka but she still kept her assumed Polish name, Hania.

29. Celebration
30. Displaced persons

We slept together on a big bed. Her brother used a mattress on the floor. It was a very small room, but we managed to stay out of each other's way since we all left for our jobs at different times.

MIGRATION TO SWEDEN, APRIL 1946; THEN TO USA IN JULY 1948

EARLY IN 1946 I VISITED the Swedish consul in Warsaw. He asked all kinds of questions and finally told me that before he could give me a transit visa to Sweden, my father would have to deposit one thousand dollars with the government of Sweden to guarantee that I would not become a burden to them. I telephoned my father and he paid the security. On the fifth of April I left for Sweden and arrived there on April 6, 1946.

I had been in Poland for almost a year. I had returned in May of 1945, and it was now April 1946.

I traveled to Sweden by train and ferry. I waited on a long line to purchase my ticket. It was an express bound for Gdansk where the train would be transferred to a ferry. The woman behind me in line was also bound for Sweden, probably for the same reason as mine. Since neither of us had too much money, we decided then and there to share a sleeper. Her name was Fini and she was a very nice lady, completely different from me. I was on the go all the time, always busy. She was subdued and quiet and I think, older than I. I believe that she had also been married before the war and had lost her husband and family.

The Baltic Sea was turbulent, and we had a very rough crossing. It was the beginning of April with March-like weather. Fini was very sick but I was well and we survived. We arrived in Malmö where we transferred to a Swedish train. From there we traveled cross-country to Stockholm, arriving at night. By the time we arrived in Stockholm, we decided to share a room, and eventually we became good friends. A member of a Jewish social service organization was waiting for us. They had apparently been notified of our arrival.

Sweden had remained neutral throughout World War II. But they did allow the German troops to cross their country in order to reach Norway. After the war, Sweden and the Swedish people did a lot for the Jewish survivors.

On arrival in Stockholm, I was greatly impressed with the helpfulness of the people. The railroad station was beautiful. The lady who met us spoke Swedish and a little English, but not Polish. Knowing some English I attempted to communicate with her. The interesting thing about many Swedes was that they were also fluent in German, but no one wanted to use it now. I spoke German to get around; the Swedes would listen, and understand. This woman arranged to rent a room for us.

On a lighter note, when we arrived in Stockholm I noticed a variety of posters and signs on the station walls warning people not to smoke, or spit. In Swedish the word forbidden is spelled *Forbjuden*. All I could see was *juden*. When I saw this I froze. I had left Poland and Germany. Now here in Sweden they still had something to say about the *Juden* [Jews]. But she explained, No, it doesn't mean *Juden* . . . it is *forbjuden,* which means forbidden. That was my first misunderstanding of a Swedish word.

Our small hotel was located in the center of the city but on a side street. By the time the woman had cleared our papers, directed us to our room, and settled us in, we were tired and fell asleep the moment we lay down on the bed. I woke in the morning to the sound of children's voices playing in the street. For a moment I didn't know where I was, and that was the first time I realized that when kids play and tease each other, they use a kind of international sing song, "Nah, nah, nah, nah-nah-nah." I thought, "Where am I?" I sat up, looked around and realized where I was when I saw Fini sleeping in the next bed. The voices of the children playing downstairs assuaged some of the strangeness I was feeling.

When I arrived in Sweden, I thought that I would be leaving for the United States immediately, but I remained there for almost two and a half years.

As I began to explore the possibility of emigrating to the United States, I realized that even though I had a father in New York, I would have to wait my turn since I was not a minor. I was advised to apply for an entry visa just as all the others did who had relatives in the United States. I was devastated when I learned that I might have to wait a long time. The Swedish Embassy became a meeting place for all of us who wanted to go to America. The American Joint Distribution Committee was another agency where we gathered for information and rumors about the latest developments.

As time moved on, I started thinking about continuing my schooling. I could have enrolled in the university in Sweden. Since I still believed that I would be going to America soon, I gave up that idea. Those who qualified could gain easy admission to the university, as the Swedish government made available a variety of special scholarships for concentration camp survivors.

During the summer of 1946 my roommate and I, as well as another family from Warsaw whom we met in our hotel, rented a place in Stortop, a small village just outside of Stockholm. After we returned from Stortop, I met Zosia whom I knew in Auschwitz. She was married now and was attending the university with her husband Gerszon. Towards the end of that year I learned some of the language. I entered a comptometry school so that I could learn a vocation.

In the meantime, my father was sending me one hundred dollars a month, which was a large sum of money for that time, especially since I didn't require much. Most of our co-survivors didn't need a great deal as long as we had shelter and something to eat and to wear.

At the beginning of 1947 we had to move out of the hotel. Fini left Stockholm and I rented an apartment with some other friends in Enskede. It was a huge place in a newly developed section of Stockholm. Our apartment became a meeting place for those who had nowhere to go. They would stay until they decided what to do. When we had money, our meals were better and we would all go to the theater. When our funds were low we ate less and did without the entertainment. It was an exciting time. We were rebuilding our lives. Stockholm was a beautiful city with many opportunities for those who really wanted to improve themselves. Money could be borrowed and college tuition could be provided. Free vocational training, health care, and jobs were available, as well as the privilege of settling in this progressive country.

During one of my periodic visits to the American Embassy, I learned that there was a shortage of female Hebrew teachers in the United States at the time. Consequently any applicant trained in this field could obtain a visa almost immediately. I wrote to my father and within several weeks I received word that they were working on securing official papers authorizing my entry into the United States as a Hebrew teacher. While my family was doing this in America I gathered information in Stockholm. Through the grapevine I heard that the American Ambassador was very selective about issuing teachers' visas. He would arrange a brief testing procedure during which the applicant was asked to translate a Hebrew text, which he checked out from a Swedish translation.

I also learned that by bribing some inside people one could learn in advance which passage would be used by the Ambassador for the examination. I discovered just in time, that the Ambassador was also very careful in verifying the degree of education the applicant had, and the teaching experience of the applicant. Having realized that, considering my age, I would not qualify, I quickly wrote to my father and requested that at least three years be added to my age in order to fit all the necessary education and experience. I also wrote to my friends in Poland for a corrected birth certificate. This was easily accomplished when one had friends in high places, or two witnesses to corroborate one's claims.

By the time all of the papers arrived I found that a couple of girls who left for America using this plan revealed to some disguised government official how they faked their way through the entire process. Subsequently, all those who planned to go as teachers were notified that the teachers' preferential quota was permanently closed. I was extremely upset because I was next in line. It was after this plan failed that I enrolled in school, received my diploma as a comptometrist and then started on a full time job, Monday through Saturday noon, in a large business office.

Despite the failure of my attempt at going as a teacher, I still visited the American Embassy at least once or twice a week, to gather gossip and new ideas. In early 1948 I learned that Canada was accepting survivors without much bureaucracy. I wrote to my father and within weeks I received documents from some new-found relatives in Canada. I established contact with the Canadian Consul's office and was told that my papers were in order. I would be called very soon.

While I was anxiously awaiting news from the Canadian Consul's office I became very ill. My doctor could not bring my high fever down. One evening, without being asked, the physician came to the house to check on me. Obviously he had some suspicion, which was well founded. During his examination he asked me to nod my head. I couldn't, and he immediately called for an ambulance, suspecting polio. I refused to go to the hospital. I was paranoid about this illness, about the possibility of becoming crippled and confined to a wheelchair. I also remembered how at one time an entire transport of Jews from Holland was sent directly to the ovens because the Germans insisted that someone had polio. I resisted strenuously until the paramedics threatened to put me in a straitjacket. All of my friends were very supportive outwardly, but truthfully they were worried that I would not make it.

In the hospital I was admitted to the communicable diseases ward. A whole team of doctors came to examine me. I argued with them about the diagnosis. I jumped out of bed in an act of sheer bravado and tried to do all sorts of calisthenics to prove that my spine was not stiff. Eventually I was diagnosed as having spinal meningitis. I was a cooperative patient and my progress was visibly apparent almost immediately. Part of the rapid improvement was related to the fact that while I was in the hospital I received an appointment to call on the Canadian Consul for my visa. My friends kept this news from me for a while, but eventually I was given the letter. I discussed this with my physician who was rather skeptical, but it was three weeks away and he took a wait-and-see attitude. When the time came the doctor allowed me to take a taxi to keep the appointment. A friend of mine accompanied me. I was quite anxious and nervous, but I was also determined. The

Canadian Consul, unlike the American one, was kind and sympathetic. The procedure was not complicated. My application was processed and I was promised an entry visa, and soon received it. I returned to the hospital and asked to be discharged. A few days later I went home, fully recovered and rehabilitated.

But I still wanted to go to the United States. With this in mind I visited the American Embassy. When I learned that the American Consul was away on vacation and his assistant, a Swede, was in charge, I was delighted. The Vice-Consul turned out to be sympathetic. He approved my American transit visa. When I went to the airline office to change my itinerary to include a stop in New York, no one believed that I had received permission to stop over in America because this was just not done at that time. They called the Consul's office to confirm that I was telling the truth.

I also asked for a week's stopover in London. I felt that Europe would be a place to which I would never wish to return, and since I always fantasized about London and its theaters and art galleries, this was my last opportunity to visit them.

My father was quite upset about this plan. He could not understand why I did not choose to leave Europe as soon as I could. He was glad however, that I did get a transit visa to the United States.

London was a little disappointing; it was bombed out. I wanted very much to see that which was no longer accessible, but I loved the city nevertheless.

On the way to the States we developed engine trouble and we were laid over in Prestwick for twenty-four hours. I called my father to tell him of the problem. Because of the delay, we arrived at Idlewild Airport at two a.m. We flew over New York for more than an hour waiting for landing clearance.

It was July 29, 1948. Waiting for me at the airport were my father, two uncles, and their wives and my cousin Tillie and her husband Jack. The reunion with my family was memorable. We cried, laughed, hugged, kissed, and talked, ad infinitum.

Postscript

I HAD MY FIRST TASTE of freedom after I arrived in Sweden in 1946. Throughout my stay in that country, the people were friendly, hospitable, and anxious to extend a helping hand to all survivors of the concentration camps. The open and warm reception, the amiable people, and the beautiful surroundings were a true feast for our souls and our eyes. For me this did not seem the end of the road. My goal was to reach America and have a reunion with my father. It was not until our plane touched down at Idlewild Airport that I knew that the many dreams I had during my years of enslavement in the ghettos or in the camps, had finally been realized.

My excitement about coming to America and meeting my father and my family again was marred by a number of difficulties I encountered in clarifying my immigration status. I came to this country to join my father, but according to the law I was too old to qualify for the preferential quota for parents and children. Thus, my initial exuberance about being a free person in a free country was subdued. I was very disappointed. For months on end, I was directed to file petitions for permission to remain in America. I suffered many rejections; I filed and refiled several appeals. I was interviewed by a number of important officials, who made many promises, but took no action.

In the interim, I tried to lead as normal a life as possible, working during the day and attending college classes in the evening. Throughout this period, my lawyer continually warned me to be careful about the people with whom I associated, the gatherings I attended and the courses I studied in college. This happened during the McCarthy era. I was told that the slightest deviation from prescribed behavior might militate against me.

I enrolled for a philosophy course in which Marx's writings were required reading. My lawyer suggested that I drop the course. I refused to do so. He then warned me not to purchase the book, or borrow it from the public library. I asked my teacher to excuse me from this part of the course. Instead, she offered to lend me her own copy. I wrapped the volume in a brown paper bag and read it at night at home, rather than in the subway on my way to work.

Eventually, my petition to remain with my father, who by then had suffered his second heart attack, was granted and there began a new series of interviews and lengthy questionnaires. When this was over two immigration agents or FBI men visited several of my neighbors, and finally came to inspect my home. This visit was not prearranged; it took place during the day while I was at work. My friend Gina from Auschwitz also emigrated to the United States and was living with us at the time. She was home, and was subjected to a great deal of questioning. She later told me that while one of the agents kept her busy, the other was carefully checking all the books (shades of the horrors of the past!). I was glad that I was not at home, but I was quite upset.

The final approval of my stay in this country came a few weeks after this inspection. In April of 1954, I was sworn in as an American citizen. This was the day that I finally and unconditionally felt free.

I HAVE BEEN ASKED what happened to everyone. I am now a retired social worker in the United States. My parents, who were very dear to me, are gone. My mother, I was told, died of starvation in a concentration camp. My father came to the United States after a brief stay in Bolivia. He made his living here as a baker. After I joined him here in 1948, we lived together until his death of heart failure in 1955.

My maternal grandmother, whom mother and I rejoined in Chelm after our return from Warsaw, died several months later of typhus.

My paternal grandmother, who was seventy-two years old at the time, died in Chelm early in 1942. We were all at her bedside, and we were convinced that she willed herself to die, so as to avoid being included in the anticipated deportation from Chelm of all Jews aged forty-five and above. During her last days, she expressed remorse that mother and I had been thwarted in going to Australia. She was buried in the cemetery in Chelm. All family members and a few old and dear friends attended her funeral.

Both my grandfathers died before I was born.

My mother, an only child, had many aunts, uncles, and cousins in Chelm, Rejo-wiec, Zamosc, Kazimierz, Lublin, and Warsaw. I know of none who survived. My attempts to locate my maternal family after the war were unsuccessful.

My father had three married sisters and a brother in Chelm. His brother was the first of the Berland family to be shot by the Germans during the famous forced march of all the Jewish elders from Chelm on December 1, 1939. Of the sisters, brothers-in-law, and their children, only one survived: the brother-in-law who had gone to Russia, and who later wanted me to help him regain family property. He then went to Israel and started a family there. He died in the late 1970s.

My friend Emma, who walked out of Birkenau with me, remained with me in Oberaltshadt, the work camp. We separated after liberation, and lost contact with each other.

The three sisters, Tania, Lusia, and Gina (these are not their real names), whom I befriended in Birkenau and with whom I was reunited after the war in Lodz, left Poland for the DP camps in Germany soon after I left for Sweden. Lusia, her husband, and Gina arrived in the United States a year before I did. They became friends with my father. Tania and her husband could not get to the United States. They went to Canada instead. We maintain contact. Gina and I see each other and speak on the telephone regularly. I have little contact with Lusia, the middle sister and her family. They live out-of-state and are very active in matters related to the Holocaust.

Fini, who entered Sweden with me, left Stockholm for Vienna, where she met and married a man she had known before the war. In 1947 she gave birth to a baby. We corresponded for a while.

For many years, I remained in touch with the Loho family, whom I revisited in Cracow in 1945. Mr. and Mrs. Loho passed away. The two youngsters, Andrew and Jadwiga, got married and formed their own families. In the sixties, Andrew was quite ill; he needed medication that could only be gotten in this country; I had the prescription filled here, and sent it on. Their mother, the roentgenologist, was not in very good health when I heard from them last some time in the late 70s.

My extended family in this country consists of cousins who were born here or who came here before World War II. My aunts and uncles who migrated to the United States before the Second World War are gone now.

I am the only Holocaust survivor among them.

Samantha Sierra

After the war, Felicia Berland Hyatt returned to Poland and then went to Sweden for two and one half years. She finally arrived in the United States in July 1948. In September, she began working in a jewelry house as a shipping and billing clerk and later as a stock control clerk. She then enrolled in an evening class in English at City College in New York. With the encouragement and assistance of her English teacher, she entered Brooklyn College, continuing to work during the day and to study in the evening. In June of 1956, she was graduated from Brooklyn College with honors.

She enrolled in the Social Work graduate program at the Adelphi University School of Social Work, where she was awarded the Master's Degree in Social Work in 1959.

Her marriage to Joseph Hyatt in 1966 ended in divorce in 1977.

She worked for the Jewish Child Care Association for many years, until her retirement in 1983, devoting her career and her attention to people who need assistance, with a special focus on children. She served as a therapist, she trained students, and also administered the psychiatric clinic.

Though retired, she continues to work in the helping fields, contributing her services to three mental health agencies.